Life Care

Understanding how the human body works is an important part of diagnosing and treating problems and diseases. This module looks at…

- medical assessments
- testing health and fitness
- diagnosis and treatment
- the breathing system
- the reproductive system.

Health Organisations

Many different organisations need to work together to ensure effective life care (care that covers all aspects of health and fitness) for patients and clients.

Whether the organisations operate locally, nationally or internationally, they are regulated to ensure that they carry out their roles to a high standard.

Examples of local organisations include local health centres, hospitals, fitness centres, opticians and ambulance centres.

Local health centres provide medical treatment for members of the community. Treatments may be free (as part of the National Health Service, NHS) or paid for by the individual (private healthcare). Some of the services available include…

- asthma clinics
- blood pressure monitoring
- cervical smears
- child health
- counselling
- diabetes clinics
- family planning (contraception)
- maternity care
- medical examinations
- minor surgery
- travel vaccinations
- ultrasound certification
- vasectomy.

Fitness centres provide a range of equipment and classes that exercise different parts of the body, and have various exercise programmes that can be adjusted to suit the needs of different people. Fitness centres are available across the country and are used for a variety of reasons, for example…

- to lose weight
- to improve levels of fitness
- to increase muscle mass.

A National Health Service

A national health service makes health care available to all of its citizens, and can provide specialist care if it is not available locally. The management needs to monitor national trends in public health (e.g. flu outbreaks), plan suitable health care, and allocate resources (medical and support staff, equipment, medicines, etc.) appropriately where and when they are needed.

> Managing how resources are allocated is not an easy task for a national health service. There are often tensions between different services, and difficult decisions have to be made about how and where funds are spent.
>
> Money is needed for administration and for the maintenance of buildings and facilities owned by the health service as well as for practitioners. All these needs must be carefully balanced; if one area is under-funded then the whole service could suffer.

Practitioners

Practitioners are people with special training, often scientific or medical. They help people to maintain and improve their health and fitness. Examples of practitioners include doctors, registered nurses, fitness instructors, nutritionists, pharmacists and opticians.

A **registered nurse** plans care for people with acute illnesses and teaches them how to stay healthy or cope with their illness. With instructions from the doctor they may administer medication, treatments and injections or take blood tests and other tests. They also observe patients for physical, mental, social and emotional changes; record changes as a result of reactions to drugs; check vital signs (e.g. temperature, pulse rate, blood pressure); and maintain health records.

A **fitness instructor** is trained to plan a programme of exercise to meet the needs and ability of an individual client. They will keep records of the training programme and take account of any medical issues.

Regular Contact

It is an advantage to have regular contact between a patient / client and a practitioner. It gives the practitioner the opportunity to become familiar with the medical history and background of the patient, and the patient will feel more comfortable and reassured if they see the same practitioner each time.

Personal Qualities

Health and fitness practitioners need to…

- develop a detached yet personal relationship with the client – not becoming too friendly
- be able to make judgements about what to do if the client's statements conflict with other evidence
- be able to work as a team
- consider their patient's whole life, e.g. his / her family, where he / she works and lives, etc.
- have empathy, patience, tact, and a manner which encourages confidence and trust from the patient / client
- be able to communicate effectively, e.g. listen, ask questions, explain and seek clarification by reinterpreting a client's statements
- understand how the human body works in order to correctly assess the health of the person and suitability of their treatment.

Discussing Health Issues

It is extremely important that health issues are brought to the public's attention through education and public information programmes.

If people are kept well informed about health risks and methods of keeping healthy, many illnesses or outbreaks of disease can be prevented.

> Although health education and public information programmes are expensive, if successful they could prevent illness and disease in the future and, in the long term, money would be saved. Therefore, they can be cost effective.

Life Care

Medical History Assessment

A patient's medical or lifestyle history needs to be disclosed before the start of any treatment or exercise programme.

This is to ensure that the treatment suggested for the patient is effective and will not make the problem worse or trigger any other problems. There are several factors that a practitioner needs to be aware of:

Alcohol consumption – high levels of alcohol consumed on a regular basis can cause physical problems. Body weight can increase to unhealthy levels, and the kidneys and liver can be damaged. Some medicines can also have an adverse effect if they are taken with alcohol.

Tobacco consumption – there are many disorders and diseases directly related to smoking, such as lung cancer, bronchitis and emphysema. Smokers also have a higher risk of developing heart disease and high blood pressure.

Symptoms – (visible or noticeable effects on the body), are usually noticed by the patient and can be used by a practitioner to identify the problem.

Previous treatments – if a patient returns repeatedly with the same symptoms, he/she might require a different diagnosis or might need to be sent to a specialist for further investigation.

Current medication – different medicines can sometimes conflict with one another, e.g. medicines combined together could cancel each other out, be harmful, or have a stronger effect on the body.

Level of physical activity – in general terms, the more exercise a person takes the healthier they will be. Lack of exercise can lead to depression, anxiety, obesity, tiredness, weak bones and problems with sleeping and concentration.

Family medical history – some medical conditions can be genetic (inherited), therefore, it is important to know the patient's family history as there may be other family members who have had the same condition and treatment for it.

A patient must be properly assessed before any diagnostic tests are carried out, to ensure that the test will not make the patient's condition worse. The risk of carrying out the test or procedure must be assessed and balanced against the advantages of making a diagnosis or being able to treat or reduce the symptoms.

For example, if a patient has a suspected peanut allergy, it would be very dangerous to ask the patient to eat a peanut to test for the allergy.

There are other less life-threatening tests that can be carried out instead, e.g. a scratch test, where minute nut traces are placed on the patient's skin in a droplet of water. A sterile needle is then used to scratch the skin through the liquid drop. If the skin reddens and blisters round the scratch, it indicates that the patient is allergic to nuts.

Testing Health and Fitness

Basic information about a person's state of health and / or fitness can be collected in a baseline (initial) health or fitness assessment.

Pulse Rate

The pulse is normally recorded as beats per minute (bpm). To take a pulse rate, press firmly but gently on the artery in the wrist or arm with the index and middle fingertips. The number of beats of the pulse is counted for 60 seconds. The average pulse rate is 60–80 beats per minute.

Blood Pressure

Blood pressure relates to the pressure of the blood against the walls of the arteries, and it results from two forces:

- Pressure from the heart as it pumps blood into the arteries and through the circulatory system.
- Pressure from the force of the arteries as they resist the blood flow.

There are, therefore, two numbers associated with blood pressure. The higher (systolic) number represents the pressure as the heart contracts (beats) to pump blood to the body. The lower (diastolic) number represents the pressure when the heart relaxes between beats. The systolic pressure is always stated first and the diastolic pressure second, e.g. a blood pressure of 118 over 76 means systolic 118 over diastolic 76. An average blood pressure is 128/80 mmHg.

Blood pressure can be measured using a sphygmomanometer or electronic sensor.

Temperature

Body temperature is measured in degrees Celsius (°C). The average body temperature is 37°C. A reading can be taken by placing...

- a sterile clinical thermometer into the mouth
- an electronic sensor thermometer in the ear
- a liquid crystal thermometer onto the forehead.

Gender

Males and females differ physiologically so calculations need to be made according to gender.

Pulse Rate

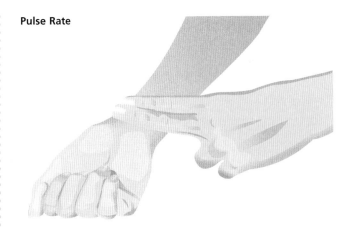

Blood Pressure – Sphygmomanometer

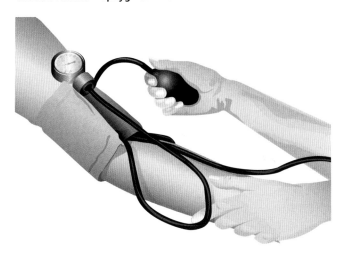

Temperature – a liquid crystal thermometer

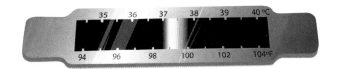

Gender

Life Care

Testing Health and Fitness (cont.)

Age

As a person gets older, his/her body ages and may become weaker or less efficient at carrying out certain processes.

Aerobic Fitness

Aerobic fitness is the ability to sustain work for prolonged periods. It can be measured by monitoring the heart rate whilst exercising for a set time period. The recovery rate – the time it takes for the heart rate to return to its resting rate after exercise – indicates aerobic fitness.

Height and Body Mass

A patient's height and mass are used to determine their Body Mass Index (BMI), a guideline which helps identify whether a patient is a healthy mass. It can be calculated using the following formula:

$$\text{Body Mass Index} = \frac{\text{Body mass (kg)}}{\text{Height}^2 \text{ (m}^2)}$$

Example

A girl is 1.85m tall and weighs 90kg. What is her BMI?

$$\text{Body Mass Index} = \frac{90}{1.85^2} = \textbf{26.3}$$

N.B. A healthy BMI is between 18.5 and 25.

It can be seen from the body mass graph below that she is slightly overweight.

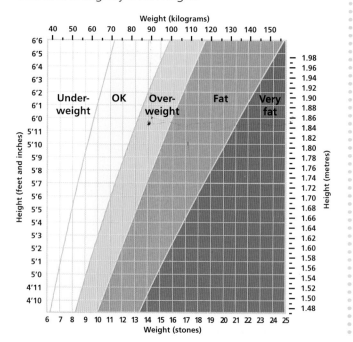

Test Results

There could be many explanations for a person's test results differing from the average:

- A **higher than average pulse rate** could be caused by recent exercise, a panic attack, anxiety (worry) or a heart disorder.
- A **weak pulse rate** could be due to low blood pressure, shock or a heart disorder.
- A **higher than average temperature** could indicate an infection or heat stroke.
- A **lower than average temperature** could be caused by hypothermia.

Recording Information

A person's personal medical or fitness information must be recorded, stored and made available to other people on the health or fitness practitioner's team. This is for the patient's benefit – if the practitioner is unavailable, then another practitioner can read the patient's notes and continue the treatment without having to start the diagnosis from the beginning.

It is also important to store information in case anything happens to the patient in the future. If necessary, records can be checked to see if there were any errors in diagnosis so that procedures can be changed. In the very rare cases that a practitioner does not follow procedures, the records can then be used as evidence to prosecute.

Blood and Urine Samples

Doctors will often require more detailed information about a patient's condition than the baseline assessment provides.

This can be gained by analysing blood, looking for infection, analysing chemicals in the body or using medical imaging techniques. Some tests are more expensive to carry out than others.

Small samples of blood and urine can be easily collected and then analysed in a laboratory.

> HT Other samples that can be taken for analysis include saliva, tissue sections, faeces and pus.

Blood Samples

A blood sample can be taken in the following way:

1. The skin is wiped with an antiseptic wipe in order to kill any harmful microorganisms.
2. A sterile syringe needle is inserted into a vein (usually in the arm), taking care to avoid the valves.
3. The vacuum inside the syringe draws the required volume of blood in, and a preservative maintains the blood under the right conditions for testing.

The blood sample can then be tested for dissolved chemicals, or smeared onto a slide to observe and count the red and white blood cells and platelets.

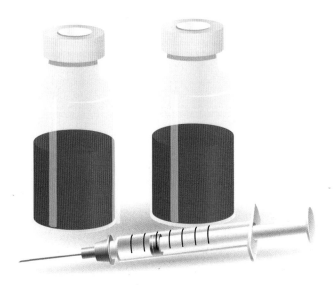

Urine Samples

Test sticks can be used to take urine samples. The sticks contain a range of chemicals or enzymes which are able to detect different substances and change colour to indicate their presence and levels. The colour can then be matched against a colour chart to give a diagnosis.

The advantages of these sticks are that they are easy to use and unlikely to cause an infection. However, they may not be sensitive enough to detect many different colour changes as they require a visual reading (and everyone's vision is slightly different).

A urine sample can be tested for the presence of nitrite (bacteria), protein, glucose (if a patient is suffering from diabetes), or hormones (to see if a patient is pregnant).

> HT In a urine sample the presence of the hormone hCG (human chorionic gonadotrophin) indicates that a woman is pregnant.

Analysing Samples

After blood and urine samples have been taken, they can be analysed to diagnose a condition or illness.

Substance Found in Blood Sample	Diagnosis
Too much glucose	Could indicate diabetes
Too little haemoglobin	Could indicate anaemia

Examples

Substance Found in Urine Sample	Diagnosis
Protein	Could indicate kidney damage or disease
Blood	Could indicate a disease of the kidneys, the urinary system or the bladder

Life Care

Medical Imaging

Medical imaging techniques are non-invasive methods of seeing inside the body and can provide both structural and functional information.

X-rays can be used to see if a bone is broken or if something is inside the body that should not be (e.g. something that has been accidentally swallowed).

The X-ray image below shows a fracture of the fibula (a leg bone). The patient's leg may appear to be normal but it could be very painful, particularly when the leg is moved.

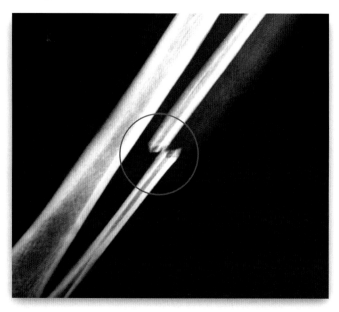

Ultrasound is most commonly used to see the developing fetus in a pregnant woman. The ultrasound image below shows a developing fetus at five months. At this age, some recognisable features can be seen.

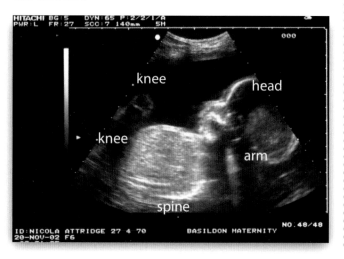

Computed Tomography (CT)

CT scans use special X-ray equipment to obtain image data from different angles around the body. A computer processes the information to show a cross-section of body tissues and organs. CT imaging is particularly useful because it can show several types of tissue – lung, bone, soft tissue and blood vessels – with great clarity.

These scans can be used to help diagnose problems such as cancers, cardiovascular disease, infectious disease and musculo-skeletal disorders.

Positron Emission Tomography (PET)

PET scans produce 3-D images. They can be used to take images of the brain or the whole body which are used to detect a variety of diseases, e.g. cancer.

PET scans of the heart can be used to determine blood flow to the heart muscle and help evaluate signs of coronary artery disease.

Magnetic Resonance Imaging (MRI)

MRI scans are a fairly new technique that use magnetic and radio waves to provide clear pictures of parts of the body that are surrounded by bone tissue, e.g. the brain and spinal cord.

An MRI scan gives very detailed pictures so it can be used to detect tumours (abnormal growths) in the brain, or to see if a tumour has spread. It can also be used to focus on other details in the brain, e.g. it is possible to find out if the brain tissue has suffered a lack of oxygen after a stroke.

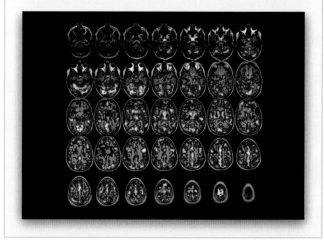

Treatments

All treatments carry some risk; there is the possibility that the treatment could cause further harm. A treatment can also have side effects which have to be weighed up against its potential benefits. Drugs manufacturers in the United Kingdom are required by law to state all known side effects on the packaging.

Before a patient is given, or undertakes, a medical treatment, their informed consent (agreement) needs to be obtained. This means making the patient aware of the risks and likelihood of success so that they can make a decision about whether they want to go ahead with the treatment.

Treatments are used to achieve an agreed target. Different treatments may require different solutions, for example...
- increased fitness could solve a problem or cure an illness
- a period of recovery may be needed in order to return to a normal level of health
- rehabilitation may be needed, e.g. learning how to walk again after an accident.

Symptoms and the Problem

There is a difference between treating the symptoms and curing the problem.

Symptoms are the result of an illness or disorder. It is possible to treat the symptoms so that they disappear, but this does not necessarily mean that the cause of the problem has been removed. With the cause of the problem remaining, the symptoms could then re-occur in the future.

For example, a patient sees an osteopath (a bone specialist) because of regular lower back pain. The osteopath can massage the back which can treat the symptoms and relieve the pain. However, this will not cure the cause of the back pain, e.g. poor posture. To cure the problem the patient may need to change his / her posture and the way he / she stands and moves.

Emergency Treatment

In the casualty department of a hospital it is vital that patients are seen in order of the seriousness of their condition. To decide on the order of treatment the hospital operates a policy of **triage** (which comes from the French word meaning 'to sort').

The triage nurse will prioritize patients based on how life-threatening their injuries are. For example, a person who has stopped breathing would be first, followed by a patient who is suffering severe bleeding, then someone with a broken leg, and finally minor injuries such as a cut hand.

Managing Resources

A hospital or fitness centre has to manage its facilities to ensure they are used most effectively. Money should be spent on appropriate equipment. For example, a rural hospital is unlikely to have to buy equipment needed to treat multiple victims of motorway accidents, and a small fitness centre would need less equipment than a larger one.

Many treatments are expensive. In the United Kingdom a public body called NICE (National Institute for Clinical Excellence) decides which treatments should be freely available on the NHS.

They may decide that although a drug may prolong or save lives, the financial cost of providing the drug is too high. The availability of treatments needs to be weighed against the available resources. Decisions have to be based on saving the most lives for the best cost, i.e cost effectiveness.

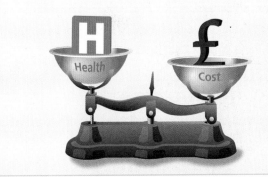

Life Care

After Diagnosis

Depending on the diagnosis, there are a number of different treatments or methods that could be used to improve health or fitness.

Surgery

Surgery can improve the health of a patient but the potential health benefits need to be weighed against the potential risks of the operation. There may be a chance of injury to healthy parts of the body, unforeseen reactions to the operation itself, or the inability to completely cure the problem.

For example, a spinal operation could be carried out to treat a severe slipped disc by removing the disc, but there is the risk of nerve damage and the possibility of paralysis. The nerve damage could also cause permanent pain – although not as intense as the pain previously felt.

Exercise Regime

An exercise regime can sometimes be the solution to a person's health problems – the patient can improve their stamina and heart rate, and lose weight.

However, the patient has to be willing to continue with the regime otherwise it will not work, so the fitness instructor has to take into account the mental attitude of the patient and ensure that achievable goals are set.

Diet

A change in diet can help a patient to lose weight, or help to improve the health of someone who may suffer from allergies or intolerances to certain foods, e.g. wheat. However, crash-dieting (losing a large amount of weight in a very short period of time) is not a healthy way to lose weight.

Drug Therapy

Drug therapy uses a course of drugs to lessen the symptoms of an illness or disorder.

Drugs can also alter the development of a disorder and lessen its effects. For example, people suffering from heart disease may be prescribed anti-cholesterol drugs to reduce their risk of heart attacks.

Public Health Campaigns

Public health campaigns are run to make the public aware of a problem. For example, obesity in the UK is increasing. The Government has run public awareness campaigns to make people aware of the issue and to suggest some possible solutions.

As a result, many people have taken note of the issue and have taken steps to change their lifestyle. Without warnings, they may have continued with their old habits without realising the risk. By running such a campaign the number of people needing medical treatment may decrease.

Physiotherapy

A physiotherapist specialises in the treatment of skeletal-muscular injuries. Physiotherapists understand how the body works and can help patients to re-train or re-use a part of their body that is not functioning properly. This is normally achieved with various exercises to strengthen muscles that may have become weakened.

There are many different exercises and it is the job of the physiotherapist to choose the best course of treatment for each patient.

For example, an injured leg could be treated by following the exercise programme below:

- Warming up the joint by riding a stationary exercise bicycle, then almost straightening and raising the leg.
- Extending the leg while sitting (a weight may be worn on the ankle for this exercise).
- Raising the leg while lying on the stomach.
- Exercising in a pool (walking as fast as possible in chest-deep water, performing small flutter kicks while holding onto the side of the pool, and raising each leg to 90° in chest-deep water while pressing the back against the side of the pool).

Monitoring and Assessing Progress

A treatment or fitness training programme needs to be monitored to check that it is having the desired effect. It can then be modified depending on the patient's progress.

A programme can be modified before completion if...
- the patient is finding the programme too hard (the problem could continue or a new injury could occur)
- the patient is finding the programme too easy (progress would be slow and the patient might not recover fast enough).

One way of monitoring progress during training is to measure the pulse rate or aerobic fitness of a patient / client (see p.7-8). A patient who is increasing his / her aerobic fitness should lower his / her heart rate and have a faster recovery rate.

After treatment or training is complete, the patient can be called back for a check-up. Questions about progress and issues are asked and sometimes tests are carried out, e.g. the pulse-rate might be checked.

Recording Progress

It is essential that accurate records are kept during treatment or fitness training because the records can be used to assess progress and determine trends. If inaccurate records are kept then progress could be slowed or even made worse.

However, progress records need to take into account the accuracy and reliability of the recording techniques.

For example, if a person is dieting they would normally weigh themselves on a regular basis, maybe every day.

However, it is usual for water levels in the body to fluctuate which can affect body weight. Measuring weight once or twice a week is a more accurate way to determine the sustained effects of a diet.

Life Care

Understanding the Body

In order to assess the health of a person, and suitability of their treatment, practitioners need to understand how the human body works.

The Heart

The heart is a muscular organ in the circulatory system which beats automatically, pumping blood around the body. The rate at which the hearts beats will vary according to stress, exertion and disease; if it stops beating completely the individual will die unless the heart can be restarted.

Most of the heart wall is made of muscle. The left side of the heart is more muscular than the right because it pumps blood around the whole body. The heart has four chambers:

- **Atria** are the smaller, less muscular upper chambers which receive blood coming back to the heart from the veins.
- **Ventricles** are the larger, more muscular lower chambers.

Valves ensure that the blood flows in the right direction (i.e. not backwards). When the heart muscles relax, blood flows into the atria through veins from the lungs and the rest of the body. The atria then contract, squeezing blood into the ventricles.

When the ventricles contract, blood is forced out of the lower chambers into two arteries which carry blood to the body and lungs. The heart muscle now relaxes and the whole process starts again.

The functioning of the heart can be studied by connecting special electrodes to the body. The electrical activity that results when the heart beats can be recorded onto a chart called an **electrocardiogram** (ECG).

Blood Vessels

There are three types of blood vessel: arteries, veins and capillaries.

- **Arteries** carry blood away from the heart towards the organs. They have thick, elastic walls to cope with the high pressure of blood coming from the heart. Substances cannot pass through the artery walls.
- **Veins** carry blood from the organs back to the heart. They have thinner, less elastic walls and they contain valves to prevent blood flowing backwards. Substances cannot pass through the vein walls.
- **Capillaries** connect arteries to the veins. They have a narrow, thin wall which is one cell thick. The exchange of substances between cells and the blood takes place here.

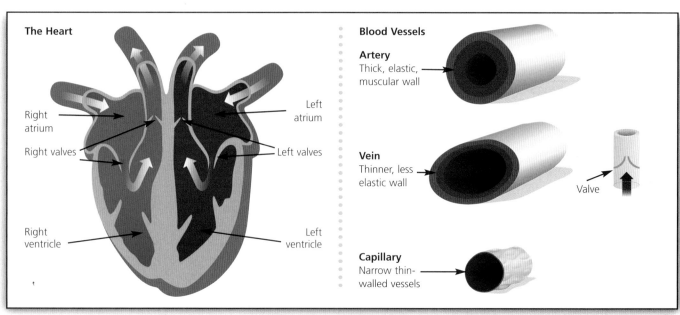

The Heart

Right atrium

Right valves

Right ventricle

Left atrium

Left valves

Left ventricle

Blood Vessels

Artery
Thick, elastic, muscular wall

Vein
Thinner, less elastic wall

Valve

Capillary
Narrow thin-walled vessels

The Human Breathing System

The most important structures in the breathing system are shown in the diagram below:

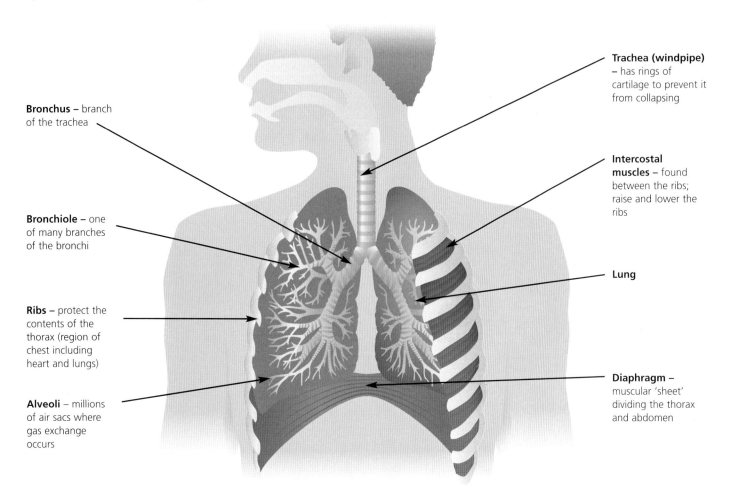

Bronchus – branch of the trachea

Bronchiole – one of many branches of the bronchi

Ribs – protect the contents of the thorax (region of chest including heart and lungs)

Alveoli – millions of air sacs where gas exchange occurs

Trachea (windpipe) – has rings of cartilage to prevent it from collapsing

Intercostal muscles – found between the ribs; raise and lower the ribs

Lung

Diaphragm – muscular 'sheet' dividing the thorax and abdomen

Ventilation

In order to move air into and out of the lungs, we need to **inhale** (take air in) and **exhale** (move air out).

To inhale, the volume of the thorax has to be increased. This is done by…
• the ribcage moving upwards and outwards
• the diaphragm becoming flatter.

To exhale, the volume of the thorax has to be decreased. This is done by…
• the ribcage moving downwards and inwards
• the diaphragm relaxing back to its original position.

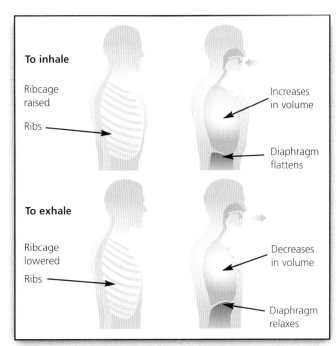

To inhale

Ribcage raised

Ribs

Increases in volume

Diaphragm flattens

To exhale

Ribcage lowered

Ribs

Decreases in volume

Diaphragm relaxes

Life Care

Blood

Blood has four components:

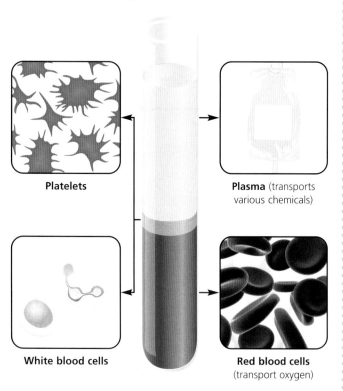

Platelets

Plasma (transports various chemicals)

White blood cells

Red blood cells (transport oxygen)

Plasma is a straw-coloured liquid that makes up about 55% of the blood volume. It transports...
- carbon dioxide from the organs to the lungs
- the soluble products of digestion from the small intestine to the organs
- urea from the liver to the kidneys.

Red blood cells transport oxygen from the lungs to the organs. They have no nucleus and are packed with haemoglobin, a red pigment. Their bi-concave shape provides a bigger surface area through which to absorb oxygen.

White blood cells have a nucleus and come in a variety of shapes. They defend the body against microorganisms; some white blood cells engulf and kill microorganisms whilst others produce antibodies to attack microorganisms.

Platelets are tiny particles found in blood plasma. They are not cells and they do not have a nucleus. When a blood vessel is damaged, platelets clump together to form a meshwork of fibres in order to form a clot and prevent blood from leaving the body.

The Human Skeleton

The human skeleton supports the body. Parts of it enclose, and therefore protect, the organs, e.g. the skull protects the brain, and the ribs protect the heart and lungs.

The skeleton also allows movement. Muscles attach to various bones which enable parts to act as levers (e.g. arms and legs).

The skeleton bones produce new blood cells (from the marrow) and store minerals (e.g. calcium, phosphorus) as well as some toxic heavy metals that the body cannot excrete (such as lead).

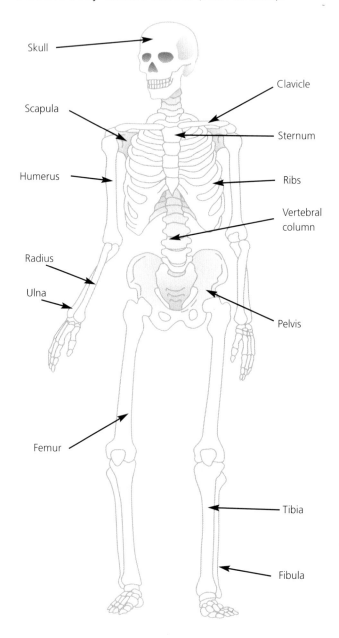

Skull
Clavicle
Scapula
Sternum
Humerus
Ribs
Vertebral column
Radius
Ulna
Pelvis
Femur
Tibia
Fibula

Ligaments, Tendons, Muscles and Bones

- **Muscle** is tissue which is designed to contract and relax.
- **Ligaments** are tough, fibrous, elastic connective tissues that connect **bones** together in a joint.
- **Tendons** are made of the same kind of tissue as ligaments but they connect muscle to bones or connect muscle to muscle.

Combining bone, muscle, tendons and ligaments together means that a joint can move easily and is able to carry out work.

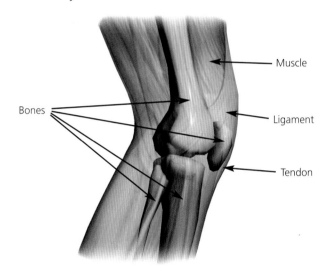

Muscle

Bones

Ligament

Tendon

The Female Reproductive System

The female reproductive system is designed to carry and give birth to babies. (See diagram at the foot of the page.)

The Menstrual Cycle

Between the ages of approximately 13 and 50, a woman is fertile and the lining of her uterus is replaced every month in preparation to carry a baby. This is called a **period**.

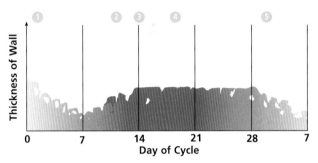

1. Uterus lining breaks down (i.e. a period).
2. Repair of the uterus wall. Oestrogen causes the uterus lining to gradually thicken.
3. Egg released by the ovary.
4. Progesterone makes the lining stay thick waiting for a fertilised egg.
5. No fertilised egg detected so cycle restarts.

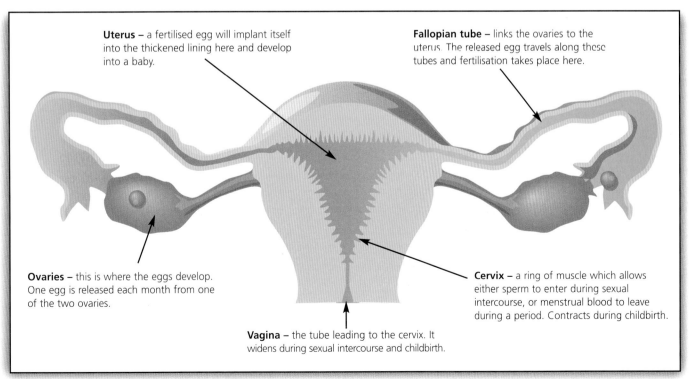

Uterus – a fertilised egg will implant itself into the thickened lining here and develop into a baby.

Fallopian tube – links the ovaries to the uterus. The released egg travels along these tubes and fertilisation takes place here.

Ovaries – this is where the eggs develop. One egg is released each month from one of the two ovaries.

Cervix – a ring of muscle which allows either sperm to enter during sexual intercourse, or menstrual blood to leave during a period. Contracts during childbirth.

Vagina – the tube leading to the cervix. It widens during sexual intercourse and childbirth.

Life Care

Fertilisation

Fertilisation occurs after sexual intercourse, when a sperm and an egg fuse together; only a single sperm can fertilise the egg. After fertilisation, the egg starts to divide and is eventually implanted into the uterus.

Pregnancy

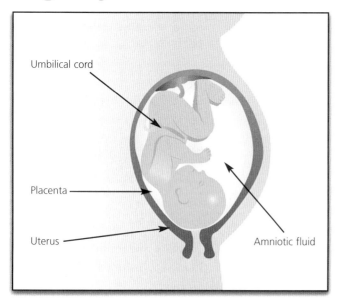

Pregnancy is the time in which the ovaries stop developing eggs, and a developing fetus is carried in the uterus.

In humans, pregnancy generally lasts around 40 weeks, and during this time there are several changes to the reproductive system:

- A **placenta**, **umbilical cord** and **amniotic sac** are produced.
- The fetus grows in length.
- The uterus expands.

The placenta is a large structure made of soft, spongy tissue which delivers food and oxygen to the developing fetus, and removes waste.

The umbilical cord contains blood vessels which carry blood between the fetus and the placenta.

The amniotic sac is the area in which the baby develops. It is filled with amniotic fluid which keeps the baby at a constant temperature and protects it from knocks and bumps.

Birth

There are three stages of labour (childbirth):

1. The contractions of the uterus cause the baby's head to align onto the cervix. The cervix dilates (widens) to 10cm and the mucus plug blocking the cervix pops out. The amniotic fluid surrounding the baby leaves the body via the vagina (known as 'waters breaking').

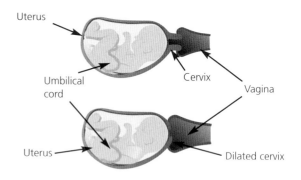

2. The contractions become stronger and occur more and more frequently. The mother has a strong urge to push and the baby is born.

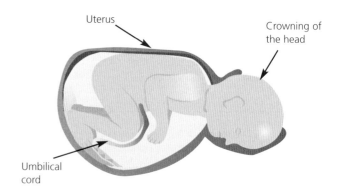

3. After the baby is born, the umbilical cord and the connected placenta detach from the uterus wall. Contractions make the cord and placenta (afterbirth) pass out of the vagina.

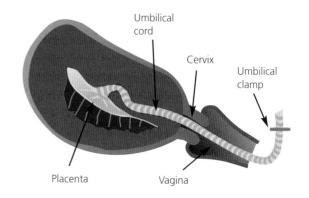

Body Temperature

The core body temperature in humans is 37°C. If it goes higher or lower than this, the systems in the body can start to fail and cause conditions such as heatstroke and hypothermia.

The skin contains temperature receptors which detect external temperature changes.

In hot conditions blood vessels in the skin dilate causing greater heat loss – more heat is lost from the skin by radiation. The skin gets redder and pores in the skin release sweat. Water, evaporating as sweat, cools the body.

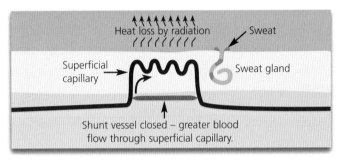

In cold conditions, blood vessels in the skin constrict reducing heat loss – less heat is lost from the surface of the skin by radiation. Skin can appear paler than normal.

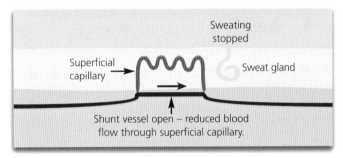

If the body gets too cold then involuntary muscle spasms take place which have the effect of warming up the muscles. This reflex is called shivering.

The Kidneys

Most people have two kidneys, one situated on either side of the spine on the back wall of the abdomen. It is the kidneys' job to control the balance of water in the body. This is achieved by adjusting the amount of urine that is released from the body.

The kidneys filter the blood to remove all waste (urea) and to balance levels of other chemicals (including water). They achieve this by…

- filtering small molecules from the blood to form urine (water, salt and urea)
- absorbing all the sugar for respiration
- absorbing as much salt as the body requires
- excreting the remaining urine, which is stored in the bladder.

The brain monitors water content constantly and causes the kidneys to adjust the concentration and volume of urine produced.

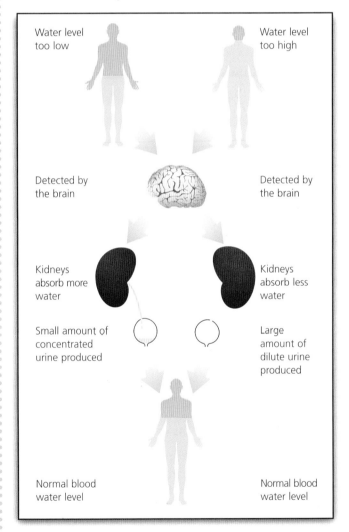

At the Bowman's capsule (a hollow, cup-shaped structure formed in the kidney), blood plasma is forced into the tubule from the blood capillaries. Blood cells and proteins are too big to pass through. Along the length of the kidney tubule certain salts and water are reabsorbed into the bloodstream.

Agriculture and Food

Module Ap2

New technologies are being developed to improve the way our food is grown and produced. This module looks at…

- flowering plants
- photosynthesis
- animal growth
- biotechnology and using microorganisms
- cloning animals and plants.

Agricultural and Food Industries

Many food products can be produced from living organisms and are harvested in different ways:

Gathered Harvests

The product is harvested but the whole organism survives, for example…

- milk from cows
- wool from sheep
- fruits and nuts from orchards and vineyards
- eggs from hens
- extracellular protein from microorganisms (e.g. chymosin used in cheese making).

Whole Organism Harvests

The whole organism is harvested and the different parts are used or consumed, for example…

- meat, leather and bonemeal fertilizer from animals
- farm crops such as sugar from sugar beet
- food from microorganisms (such as Quorn™ which is cultured from a species of fungus).

Using Organisms for Tasks

Organisms are used in many processes, for example…

- environmental management, e.g. creating areas of hedging
- waste treatment, e.g. reed beds used as a way to filter sewage
- food processing, e.g. brewing beer, making yoghurt and cheese
- to produce fuel for transport, e.g. using yeast to make ethanol.

Food Production Chain

A chain of food production shows every stage of growing, transporting, processing, storing and delivering food from the farm or factory to the home.

Example: Production of Flour

Wheat grown and harvested

Grains transported to factory

Wheat grains milled and processed into flour

Flour bagged and stored in warehouse

Bags of flour delivered to supermarket

Regulatory Organisations

Organisations have been set up in order to regulate agriculture and food production. Their purpose is to...

- protect the public's health and safety
- make sure that animals are treated humanely and that their welfare is considered
- protect the environment.

Two examples of such regulatory organisations are the Department of Environment, Food and Rural Affairs (DEFRA), and the Food Standards Agency (FSA).

Enforcement officers, such as environmental health practitioners and factory inspectors, monitor each step of the food chain and ensure that regulations are adhered to.

There are also organisations which support a particular part of the food industry, carrying out research and promoting its products. Such organisations include the Milk Development Council, the British Potato Council, the Meat and Livestock Commission, and the Agricultural Development and Advisory Service (ADAS).

The **Milk Development Council** aims to increase demand for British milk. It provides the opportunities and knowledge to help dairy farmers to improve their profits. Activities include marketing, research and development of milk, and the provision of market information.

The **British Potato Council** advises the potato industry on market trends, distributes information to the public and encourages more people to buy potatoes.

The **Meat and Livestock Commission** works with the British meat and livestock (cattle, sheep and pigs) industry to improve its efficiency and competitive position. It also tries to create markets both in the UK and abroad.

ADAS provides advice and services for environmental and rural issues.

Foods From Plants

There is a huge variety of food that can be made from plants, for example:

- Grass, hay (a mixture of dried grass and perennial plants) or silage (the fermented remains of crops) are fed to farm animals.
- Crop plants such as potatoes, lettuce and apples are eaten by people.
- Many food ingredients, e.g. flour, sugar and vegetable oils, are derived from plants.

Plants are also grown for other purposes:

- Materials, e.g. wood and paper.
- Fibres and fabrics, e.g. cotton and linen.
- Biofuels, e.g. alcohol and biodiesel.

Agriculture and Food

Flowering Plants

Stages in the life-cycle of flowering plants include:

Pollination

Pollination is the transfer of pollen (tiny egg-shaped male cells) from the stamen (male part of the flower) to the stigma (female part of the flower). Pollen can be transferred from plant to plant by insects or the wind.

Fertilisation and Production of Seeds / Fruit

The pollen fertilises the female organs (ova) and seeds are formed. The pollen grains contain the cells to form the pollen tube and sperm cells.

Dispersal of Seeds / Fruit

Once the seeds are formed, they need to be dispersed so that they have the best chance of growing into a new plant. They can be dispersed by water, wind, insects, animals, etc. For example...

- sycamore seeds have wings which enable them to travel a great distance from the parent plant
- cleaver seeds have hooks which can become attached to animals.

Germination of Seeds

The seeds begin to germinate (sprout shoots) under favourable conditions, e.g. correct temperature and correct levels of water, light, oxygen, etc. The embryonic tissues resume growth, developing towards a seedling. The part of the plant that emerges from the seed first is called a **radicle**.

The **germination rate** can be calculated by counting the difference between the number of seeds planted and the number of seeds that germinate. The rate is expressed as a percentage and gives an indication of how successfully seeds germinate. It is calculated using the following formula:

$$\text{Germination rate} = \frac{\text{No. of seeds germinated}}{\text{Total number of seeds planted}} \times 100$$

Example

Ten seeds were planted, but only one germinated. Calculate the germination rate.

Germination rate = $\frac{1}{10}$ x 100 = **10%**

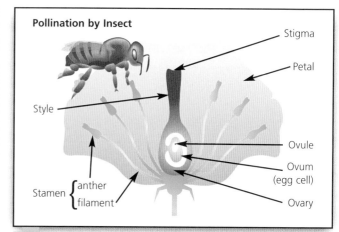

Pollination by Insect

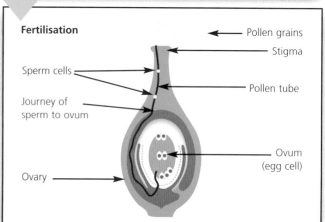

Fertilisation

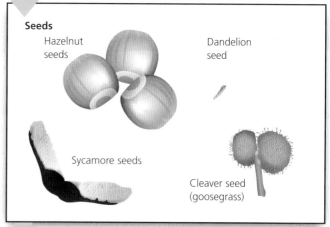

Seeds

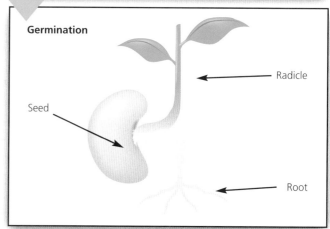

Germination

Growing Media

Three factors need to be balanced in a growing medium in order to ensure the maximum growth of plants:

- the amount of water supplied
- the source of nutrients
- the pH of the soil.

Growing plants also need to be supported. Soil or compost provides a physical support for the roots, water and nutrients.

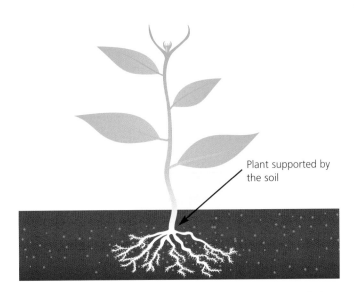

Plant supported by the soil

Some plants can be grown without soil; instead the plants are grown with their roots in a solution. This method is known as **hydroponics**.

Nutrients needed for healthy plant growth are added to the solution.

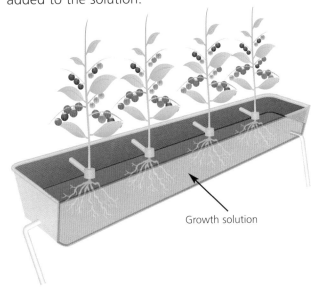

Growth solution

Photosynthesis

Green plants make their own food (glucose), using sunlight, in a process called **photosynthesis** ('making through light'). It occurs in cells that are exposed to light.

Four things are needed for photosynthesis to occur:
- light from the Sun
- carbon dioxide diffused from the air
- water from the soil
- chlorophyll in the leaves.

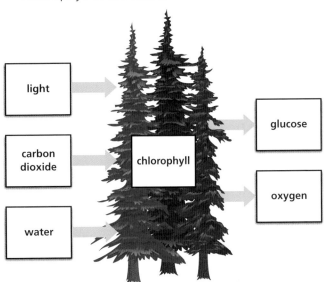

The word equation for photosynthesis is...

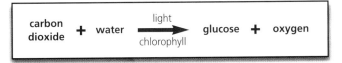

$$\text{carbon dioxide} + \text{water} \xrightarrow[\text{chlorophyll}]{\text{light}} \text{glucose} + \text{oxygen}$$

Some of the glucose produced in photosynthesis is used immediately by the plant to provide energy via respiration. However, much of the glucose is converted into insoluble starch which is stored in the stem, leaves or roots.

Factors Affecting Photosynthesis

Temperature, carbon dioxide concentration and light intensity interact to limit the rate of photosynthesis. Any one of them, at a particular time, may be the limiting factor.

Agriculture and Food

Controlling Growing Conditions

In a protected cultivation, e.g. glasshouses or polytunnels (polythene tunnels constructed over a crop), growing conditions can be controlled in order to increase the growth of crops. For example, in glasshouses the amount of carbon dioxide can be increased, and the temperature can be raised by shining light onto the ground.

Protecting Crops

Crops grown in a glasshouse can be vulnerable to attack by insect pests.

Two methods can be used to minimise crop loss due to insects:

- **Chemical pest control** – a chemical is sprayed onto the crop to kill the insects feeding on it. The pests may be killed quickly before they can damage large amounts of the crop. However, a chemical residue may remain on the plant and could be eaten by animals and enter the food chain, potentially causing harm. There is also the risk that the chemicals could be washed into surrounding streams and rivers.
- **Biological pest control** – another organism is deliberately introduced in order to eat the insect pests that are destroying the crop. The advantage to this method is that it is an environmentally friendly way of farming and leaves no chemical residue. The disadvantage is that the new insects may not eat the insect pest fast enough and some of the crop may be ruined, which reduces profits.

Measuring Crop Yields

Yields of crops such as potatoes and peas can be found by measuring the wet mass, i.e. the mass of the whole, fresh product.

> HT Dry mass is measured for crops that are stored dry (i.e. have had all water removed) such as tea, or cereal grains like wheat or barley.

Cloning Plants

Plants can be manipulated to create large numbers of genetically identical plants (clones). This is ideal for buyers as they know exactly what they are getting in terms of quality, taste and properties.

Cloning can be done in two ways:

- **Taking cuttings** – plants can be reproduced by taking a cutting and putting it in a rooting hormone which causes roots to form. Because the cutting already has a stem and leaves, it will develop into a complete new plant which is genetically identical to the parent plant.
- **Tissue culture** – if a cutting cannot be taken, cells can be taken under sterile conditions and then introduced to a medium rich in plant growth hormones. The cells act as stem cells (unspecialised cells) and are able to develop into any type of cell. Genetically identical plants are then produced from the plant that the original cells were harvested from.

Taking Cuttings

Plant from which cuttings are taken

Cuttings dipped into a rooting hormone

Roots form; new plants develop which are genetically identical to the original

Tissue Culture

Plant from which cells are taken

Cells introduced into growth medium

Plants which are genetically identical to the original plant are produced

Farming Animals

Farm animals can be used to provide various food sources and useful products, for example...

- food such as meat, eggs, milk and dairy products
- textiles such as wool and leather
- fertilizers such as manures and bonemeal.

Animals can be reared using **organic** or **intensive** farming methods.

Organic farming concentrates on the quality of a product. Organic farms do not use synthetic fertilizers and pesticides. Instead, they rely on crop rotation, crop residues, animal manures and mechanical cultivation to maintain soil productivity and to control weeds and pests. Organic farmers treat their animals with respect and farm as sustainably as possible.

Intensive farming concentrates on quantity and aims to maximise production. Intensive farms rely on the use of chemical fertilizers, herbicides, fungicides, insecticides, plant growth regulators and pesticides to increase yield.

There may be ethical issues concerning the way in which intensively reared animals are looked after. Animals can be kept in carefully controlled conditions where their body temperature and movement are limited in order to maximise growth.

Animal Growth

There are five main factors that affect animal growth.

1. **Temperature** – the animals must be kept in temperatures in which they can live comfortably.
2. **Shelter** – animals need shelter from the elements, especially during the winter months.
3. **Food** – all animals need food in order to survive. The type and variety of food eaten by the animals can affect the taste of the food produced.
4. **Water** – all animals need a constant supply of clean, fresh water in order to survive.
5. **Pests and disease** – all animals need to be healthy (protected from pests and disease) in order to produce tasty, high-quality food.

Animal Food Sources and Products

Organic Farming

Intensive Farming

Agriculture and Food

Animal Reproduction

Science and technology can be used extensively in the controlled reproduction and breeding programmes of mammals. By understanding the stages involved in reproduction, the breeding processes can be manipulated to the advantage of the farmer.

There are several main stages in the sexual reproduction process of mammals:

Formation of Gametes

Meiosis takes place in the testes and ovaries. It is a special type of cell division where the parent cell produces **gametes** (sex cells, i.e. eggs and sperm for sexual reproduction). Gametes contain half the number of chromosomes of the parent cell:

- The sperm are formed in the testes of males.
- The ova (eggs) are formed in the ovaries of females.

Fertilisation

During sexual reproduction the penis is inserted into the vagina and sperm are ejaculated. The sperm then swim to the ovum; only one sperm can fertilise the ovum.

Fertilisation occurs at the point where the nucleus from the male sperm cell joins with the nucleus from the female egg cell. The resultant cell (called a **zygote**) will then divide into further cells (an **embryo**).

Internal Development and Birth

All development takes place inside the uterus. The mother supplies the developing fetus with food via the placenta. After the gestation period (the time in which a fetus is carried inside the mother) the animal will be born. Gestation periods vary from animal to animal, for example, it is 279 days for a cow, 151 days for a sheep, 155 days for a goat and 115 days for a pig.

Growth and Development

Following birth, an animal continues to grow until it reaches its adult size. Development is dependent on the animal receiving enough food and water, being sheltered and being protected from disease and pests.

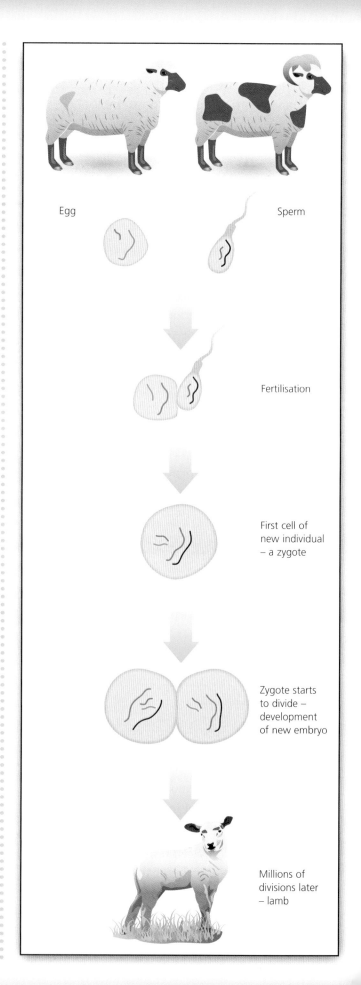

Egg

Sperm

Fertilisation

First cell of new individual – a zygote

Zygote starts to divide – development of new embryo

Millions of divisions later – lamb

Artificial Insemination

Farm animals can be artificially inseminated (i.e. fertilised using artificial means rather than through sexual intercourse). This type of controlled breeding means that parents can be selected because of their desirable characteristics, e.g. a prize bull and a heffer that produces a high yield of milk.

The timing of an animal's pregnancy can also be controlled which benefits the farmer because the same animal can produce young continuously, or produce young at a particularly convenient time.

The process of artificial insemination involves four stages:

1 Selection of animals

The parents are selected due to required characteristics, e.g. high milk production in cows. The animals do not need to be on the same farm; arrangements can be made to use sperm from a desirable animal elsewhere in the country.

2 Collection of sperm

Once the parent animals have been selected, the sperm from the male needs to be collected. Two methods include:

- The male is aroused with either a teaser female or a decoy animal. As the male tries to mount the female, breeders discreetly direct its penis into a latex collection reservoir.
- Electroejaculation, where mild electrical stimulation is applied to the accessory sex glands. This allows breeders to collect a sperm sample without a female, or decoy, being present.

3 Storage of sperm

The sperm must then be stored until it is needed. A straw containing the sperm is dipped into liquid nitrogen. The extremely low temperature, -196°C, rapidly freezes the 'sperm straw' which can then be kept in a tank until it is required.

4 Timing of sperm insertion

The sperm needs to be inserted into the chosen female at her most fertile period. The abdomen is sterilised and, if necessary, shaved. A laparoscope (a tool to see inside the body) and an inseminating pipette containing the sperm straw is inserted through two very small holes at locally anaesthetised sites. Half of the straw of semen is injected directly into each side of the uterus.

> **HT** Sometimes hormones can be given to the female to ensure that an egg is released. This means that the time of fertilisation can be controlled more accurately.

Selective Breeding

Productivity can also be increased by using selective breeding; animals with certain traits are deliberately mated to produce offspring with certain desirable characteristics. For example, some breeds of cattle have been bred to produce high yields of milk or milk with a high fat content.

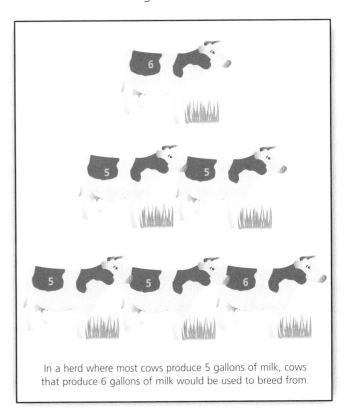

In a herd where most cows produce 5 gallons of milk, cows that produce 6 gallons of milk would be used to breed from.

Agriculture and Food

Surrogate Mothers

Biological mother (donor female)

(arrow down)

Embryo removed from the biological mother

(arrow down)

Embryo placed in the uterus of a surrogate mother

(arrow down)

Embryo develops into a fetus and is born in the normal way

Surrogate Mothers

An animal that has been treated with fertility hormones may produce more than one embryo. The spare embryo(s) can sometimes, therefore, be removed from the female and implanted into the uterus of a surrogate mother.

1. The donor female (biological mother) undergoes surgery to remove the embryo.
2. The embryo is then inserted into the uterus of the surrogate mother during an operation.
3. The embryo implants into the uterus of the surrogate mother and then develops as normal.

Microorganisms and Food

Microorganisms include yeasts, bacteria and viruses. Some microorganisms can be used to produce food, for example:

- Yeast is used in the production of bread, and alcohol (which can be used in the drinks industry or as a fuel).
- Bacteria such as *Lactobacillus* are used to turn milk into yoghurt whilst others are used to produce bread, cheese and mycoprotein.
- Microorganisms can provide enzymes such as chymosin which is used in the production of cheese. Chymosin was originally extracted from the stomachs of animals, but it can now be genetically engineered from bacteria.

However, not all microorganisms are useful in food production. Some microorganisms can spoil many products by feeding on them and contaminating them with their waste products. There are also some microorganisms which cause disease.

> HT Disease-causing microorganisms are called **pathogens**.

A Single Bacterium

Yeast

Biotechnology

Biotechnology can be used to produce food. Beer fermentation and mycoprotein (a meat substitute) fermentation are two examples.

Beer Fermentation

1. Malted barley is soaked in hot water to release the malt sugars.
2. The malt sugar solution is boiled with hops (for flavour).
3. The solution is cooled and the yeast is added to begin the process of fermentation.
4. The yeast ferments the sugars, releasing carbon dioxide (CO_2) and alcohol.
5. When the main fermentation is complete, the beer is bottled with a little bit of added sugar to provide the carbonation.

Mycoprotein Fermentation

1. A nutrient broth is added to the culture vessel.
2. A pure culture of fungus is added.
3. The fungal hyphae (string-like filaments that increase surface area) grow.
4. The fungus is harvested.
5. The cycle starts again.

Respiration

There are two types of respiration in which energy can be released from food:
- aerobic respiration
- anaerobic respiration.

Aerobic Respiration

This type of respiration releases energy through the breakdown of glucose molecules, by combining them with oxygen inside living cells. The majority of organisms respire aerobically and it is the main method of releasing energy from food. The word equation is:

$$\text{glucose} + \text{oxygen} \longrightarrow \text{carbon dioxide} + \text{water} \ (+\ \text{energy})$$

Anaerobic Respiration

This type of respiration takes place in the absence of oxygen. It is less efficient than aerobic respiration and produces less energy. The word equation for the anaerobic respiration of yeast is:

$$\text{glucose} \longrightarrow \text{alcohol} + \text{carbon dioxide} \ (+\ \text{energy})$$

Fermentation

Respiring microorganisms can be used to produce alcohol in a **fermentation** process.

There are two stages involved in brewing:

1. **Aerobic fermentation**
   - Lasts about a week.
   - Yeast is exposed to air and grows rapidly.
   - Some alcohol is produced but the majority of energy is used to produce more yeast cells.
2. **Anaerobic fermentation**
   - Lasts for weeks or months.
   - Takes place in the absence of oxygen.
   - Without oxygen, the yeast produces alcohol rather than multiplying.

Approximately 70% of fermentation takes place aerobically. The remaining 30% of fermentation takes place anaerobically.

Yogurt is made through anaerobic fermentation of the sugar lactose to produce lactic acid.

Vinegar is made by first producing alcohol (wine or cider) and then carrying out aerobic fermentation to change the alcohol into acetic acid (vinegar).

Agriculture and Food

Culturing Microorganisms

When culturing a specific microorganism it is important to ensure that aseptic techniques are used to make sure that conditions are sterile and that any unwanted microorganisms are killed.

When culturing microorganisms, it is important to understand the stages they go through during growth.

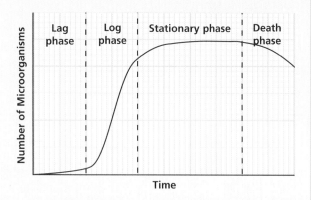

The lag phase – growth is slow as the microorganisms adapt to the new living conditions.

The log phase – the microorganisms begin to double in number every few minutes.

The stationary phase – more and more microorganisms are competing with each other for a rapidly reducing quantity of nutrients.

The death phase – toxins produced by the microorganisms build up to a very high level and, combined with the lack of resources, the population dies.

Genetic Modification

Genetically modified microorganisms can be used to produce both the food ingredients and the enzymes used in food processing.

Genetic modification is where a gene which codes for the production of a desirable protein from one organism is introduced into another organism. The genetically modified organism can now produce the protein that the original organism produced.

Genetically modified microorganisms are used in the production of insulin for diabetics. Millions of people worldwide lack the ability to produce insulin. As a result they require regular injections of insulin.

Until recently, the insulin was taken from pigs and cows. However, it is now possible to use genetically modified bacteria to produce human insulin.

DNA is the genetic material of all organisms. The DNA contains the genes which code for the particular protein that the organism needs. The proteins produced by one organism may not be produced by another.

By carrying out genetic modification, the gene that produces a protein can be inserted into another organism so that it too produces the required protein.

Once the gene has been identified it can be cut out (using special proteins which target and cut DNA). They are then inserted into the DNA of the target organism.

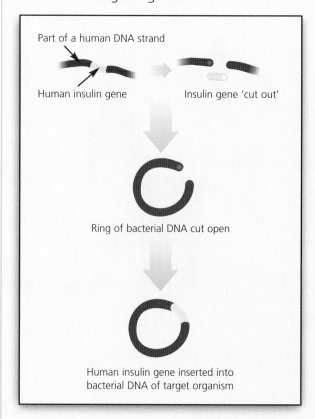

Batch and Continuous Cultures

Batch culture is the name given to a closed system culture of microorganisms with specific nutrient types, temperature, pressure, aeration (dissolved air in a liquid), and other environmental conditions. Only a few generations of microorganism are able to grow before all the nutrients are used up. This kind of culture generally takes place in a large container such as a vat.

Advantage
Easy to set up and maintain.

Disadvantage
Conditions will quickly change from the ideal due to the growth of the microorganisms.

A **continuous culture** is where microorganisms are grown in a system where the culture medium is continually replenished with fresh nutrients. The conditions (temperature, light, pressure) remain constant and microorganisms are regularly removed.

Advantage
Microorganisms can be grown over a long period of time without the conditions changing from the ideal.

Disadvantage
Expensive to set up and maintain (needs computers to monitor).

Fermenter

A **fermenter** is a controlled environment which provides ideal conditions for the microorganisms to live in, feed, and produce the proteins needed.

A fermenter enables the continuous culture of large quantities of microorganisms or their products, e.g. alcohol.

In a closed culture system, alcohol would usually build up to levels that would kill the yeast. Using a fermenter means that the alcohol can be removed regularly, allowing the yeast to continue to produce the alcohol.

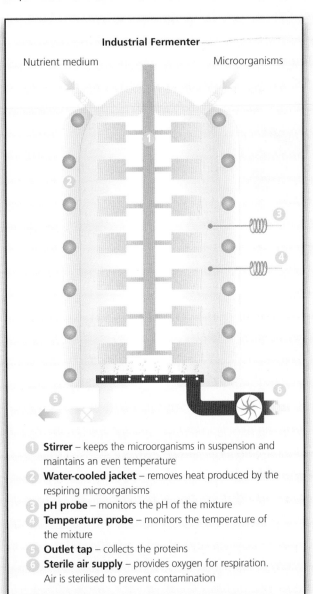

Industrial Fermenter

Nutrient medium

Microorganisms

1. **Stirrer** – keeps the microorganisms in suspension and maintains an even temperature
2. **Water-cooled jacket** – removes heat produced by the respiring microorganisms
3. **pH probe** – monitors the pH of the mixture
4. **Temperature probe** – monitors the temperature of the mixture
5. **Outlet tap** – collects the proteins
6. **Sterile air supply** – provides oxygen for respiration. Air is sterilised to prevent contamination

Agriculture and Food

Testing Quality and Safety

It is important that food and food products are tested during development. Testing can take place at different stages in the production cycle, from the initial growth of the crop plant or animal to the finished packaged product. This is to…

• prevent poor quality
• identify and correct issues before it is too late (e.g. deficiency in nutrients / minerals)
• prevent the selling of a product contaminated by toxins or harmful microorganisms.

Three types of test are used:
1 Qualitative
2 Semi-quantitative
3 Quantitative

Qualitative Test

This is where someone is trained to observe characteristics or deficiencies in the food or product. These tests are dependent upon the skills of the tester and it is, therefore, possible to have different people reaching different conclusions, for example:

• A magnesium deficiency in the soil would result in crops that had yellowing leaves. A trained observer could visually spot this, determine the cause and correct it.
• The end of beer fermentation can be observed by looking at the brew.
• The colour of dyes can be visually tested to see if they are the same colour.
• Processed food can be visually inspected to check that it reaches a required quality.

Semi-quantitative Test

This test involves both human input and the use of some equipment, for example:

• The acidity of soil can be tested using pH paper. The tester then has to visually determine the pH level by comparing it to the pH paper.
• Indicators can be used to test for the presence of bacteria. These contain a compound that changes colour when particular compounds produced by bacteria (e.g. amines) are present.
• Testing for whole cereal grains.

Quantitative Test

This test measures a given property and gives a numerical value; this is more accurate than qualitative or semi-quantitative, tests, for example:

• The acidity of soil can be tested using a pH probe. This will give an accurate result and is not dependent upon the skills of the observer.
• A hydrometer is used in brewing to determine the alcohol level.
• The percentage of seed germination can be calculated by counting the plants that have grown from the number of seeds planted.
• For food containing coloured dyes, a colorimeter can be used to determine either absorbance or transmittance at given light wavelengths. If the colour of the dye is the same then the colorimeter value will be the same.
• The amount of carbohydrate and protein in cereal grains can be measured by adding antibodies made against the carbohydrate or protein concerned. The antibodies glow when a detector is added. The amount of light given out can then be measured.

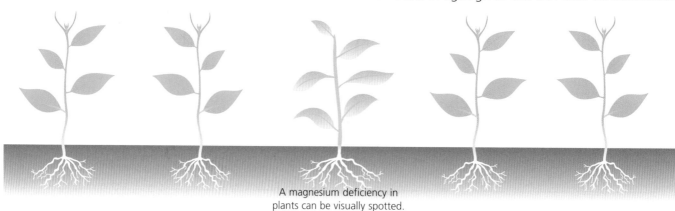

A magnesium deficiency in plants can be visually spotted.

Economics

Suppliers of food products made from living organisms operate in a market where the price of the product is determined by supply (how much is available) and demand (the quantity in which a customer wants to buy a product).

Unlike many other industries, suppliers are also affected by government intervention. The government can instigate bans (such as those that were enforced after Foot and Mouth disease entered Britain) or provide subsidies (where the supplier receives government funding so that they can offer the product at a lower price to the public).

Marketing

Marketing products is important for any organisation that depends on sales. Advertising is used to bring the product (especially new products) to the attention of potential consumers. Marketing is also needed following events where people may have been unable to buy a product due to previous government intervention (e.g. after issues with BSE in the early 1990s, advertising was needed to encourage consumers to buy British beef).

Quality of Products

Another way of establishing the quality of a product is to apply for a quality mark. A quality mark adds market value to the product as the consumer understands that the products have been produced to the highest standards of food safety or quality.

For example, to qualify for a **Lion Quality** mark on eggs, there are several standards that must be met:
- The hens must have been vaccinated against *Salmonella enteritidis.*
- The traceability of eggs must be independently audited.
- A 'best before' date must be stamped on the shell and packaging.
- There must be hygiene controls on the farms and packing stations.

Foot and Mouth Disease

Lion Quality Mark on Eggs

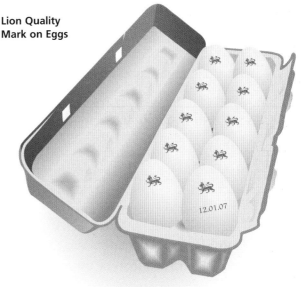

Soil Association Quality Mark on Peppers

The **Soil Association** quality mark on organic food shows that it exceeds the regulations set down in law by the Government, and meets the highest level of standards set for organically grown food.

Glossary

Aerobic Respiration – respiration using oxygen which releases energy and produces carbon dioxide and water

Arteries – vessels which carry blood away from the heart towards the organs

Artificial insemination – a method of controlled breeding without sexual intercourse

Biotechnology – any technological application that uses biological systems or living organisms for a specific use

Blood plasma – a straw-coloured liquid found in the blood

Blood pressure – the force of blood exerted on the inside walls of blood vessels

Body Mass Index (BMI) – a calculation which compares a person's mass against their height to see if he / is has a healthy mass

Bones – rigid tissues that make up the human skeleton

Capillaries – vessels that connect arteries to veins

Clone – a genetically identical copy of a plant or animal

Fertilisation – the fusion of the male nucleus with the female nucleus

Gamete – a specialised cell formed by meiosis

Genetically modified – an organism which has had its genetic make-up changed by the introduction of genetic information from another organism

Germination – the growth of a seed

Heart – a muscular organ which pumps blood around the body

Hydroponics – the method of growing plants in a solution instead of soil or compost

Intensive farming – farming that uses artificial pesticides and fertilizers, and with an emphasis on producing quantity

Ligament – tissue that connects a bone to a joint

Menstrual cycle – the monthly cycle of hormonal changes in a woman to prepare the body to carry a baby

Muscle – tissue designed to contract and relax to produce movement

Organic farming – farming without the use of pesticides and fertilizers, and with an emphasis on producing quality products

pH – a measure of the strength of an acid or alkali

Photosynthesis – the chemical process in green plants where water combines with carbon dioxide to produce glucose using light energy

Physiotherapist – a specialist in the treatment of skeletal-muscular injuries

Platelets – tiny particles found in blood plasma

Pollination – the transfer of pollen between plants in order to fertilise them

Pulse rate – the number of times a heart beats each minute in a person's body

Selective breeding – where animals are deliberately mated to produce offspring with desirable characteristics

Symptom – a visible or noticeable effect of a disease, illness or injury

Tendon – tissue connecting a muscle to a bone

Ultrasound – an imaging technique used to examine babies in the womb

Veins – vessels which carry blood from the organs to the heart

Wet mass – the mass of a whole, fresh product or plant

X-ray – an imaging technique which produces shadow pictures of bone and metal

 DNA – deoxyribonucleic acid which contains the genetic information carried by every cell
Dry mass – the mass of a dry crop
Pathogen – a disease-causing microorganism

Module Ap3

Collecting and analysing reliable scientific evidence is important at local, national and international levels. This module looks at…
- the need for scientific evidence
- imaging
- chromatography and electrophoresis
- the use of colour in analysis
- the general principles of evidence.

Scientific Expertise

People with scientific expertise are employed in jobs in many areas of society, including law enforcement, environmental protection and consumer protection. Some examples of such jobs, and the organisations in which they might work, are detailed below.

Law Enforcement

Crime scene investigators work with police to investigate serious crime (e.g. burglary, assault, murder and reckless driving). They gather and interpret information found at crime scenes (e.g. a burgled house, a site where an assault took place, etc.).

The investigator's job is to retrieve, examine and investigate physical evidence that may help to trace and convict criminals. This includes…
- taking fingerprints
- examining victims, suspects, property and clothing for traces of forensic evidence
- facial identification techniques
- collecting, recording, storing and submitting evidence.

After the investigators have gathered the evidence they will not normally have any further involvement in the case. Investigators will often work for the **Forensic Science Service (FSS)** which gathers and analyses evidence such as DNA, firearms, drugs and fingerprints. They are also involved in paternity testing, and the research and development of mobile phones and electronic technology.

Environmental Protection

The role of **environment protection officers** is very varied and can range from planning consultations to investigating pollution incidents (e.g. an oil spill). Their activities include…
- monitoring industrial sites, e.g. chemical stores
- testing pollution levels of water
- educating farmers on how to keep fertilizer records.

Officers may work for the **Environment Agency**, which collects and monitors data on environmental protection. The services undertaken by the agency include collecting air quality data to monitor climatic changes, monitoring and protecting wildlife, and ensuring that hazardous waste has been disposed of correctly.

Consumer Protection

Public analysts check to see if health and safety standards are being met. They need to have a good understanding of chemical analysis and the law, as well as being up to date with food technology. Analysts are often employed by the **Food Standards Agency (FSA)**. The FSA provides advice and information to the public and Government on food safety. It monitors nutrition and diet, handles food licensing and safety, ensures that foods are correctly labelled, and researches food-borne illnesses.

Scientific Detection

Reliable Evidence

When data is collected, it is very important that samples are representative, which is achieved by collecting multiple samples at random. The samples should be stored in a sterile container to prevent change or deterioration. The container should be sealed, labelled and stored in a safe place. If samples become contaminated, or are tampered with, then the evidence is changed and the sample is no longer reliable.

It is essential that any scientific data collected is accurate and reliable because important decisions may be based on the evidence it produces. Inaccurate or incorrect data presented in a court of law could lead to a miscarriage of justice. Many public laboratories, therefore, have a system of accreditation, for example, for reliability. Any evidence from these laboratories will be supported by the accreditation.

Using a system of **common practices and procedures**, such as ensuring that samples are not contaminated, can increase reliability since there is less room for human error and different people can repeat a test on the same sample.

Proficiency tests are carried out to check the accuracy of analytical procedures. Identical samples are sent to a group of laboratories. Each laboratory analyses the sample and returns their results. The results are then compiled into a report, which is circulated to all the participating laboratories. The tests are used to highlight laboratories that are not producing accurate results.

Good laboratory practice depends on…
- adherence to health and safety regulations
- training and continuing professional development of staff to ensure that the most up-to-date methods are used
- regular maintenance and checking of equipment and instruments.

> **HT** Regularly checking equipment ensures that systematic or random errors do not go unnoticed.

Chromatography

Chromatography is a technique used to find out what unknown mixtures are made up of.

Paper Chromatography

1. If the substance to be analysed is a solid, dissolve it in a suitable solvent (the solvent used will depend on the solubility of the substance. Some substances dissolve well in water, whilst others require a non-aqueous solvent, i.e. a solvent other than water).
2. Place a spot of the resulting solution onto a sheet of chromatography paper on the pencil line and allow to dry.
3. Place the bottom edge of the paper into a suitable solvent.
4. The solvent rises up the paper.
5. The solvent dissolves the 'spot' and carries it, in solution, up the paper.
6. The different chemicals in the mixture become separated because their molecules have different sizes and properties. The molecules that bind strongly to the paper travel a shorter distance than the molecules that bind weakly to the paper.

The chromatogram can then be compared to standard chromatograms (standard reference materials) of known substances to identify the different chemicals.

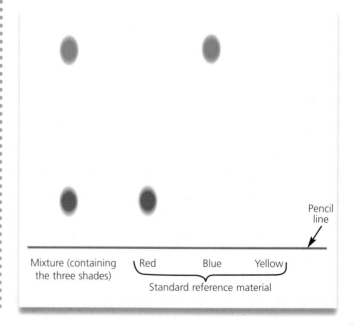

The solvent that is used to move the solution is called the **mobile phase**. The medium that it moves through (in this case, the paper) is called the **stationary phase**.

A chromatogram is formed when the chemicals in the substance come out of solution and bind to the paper, i.e. they move between the mobile phase and the stationary phase.

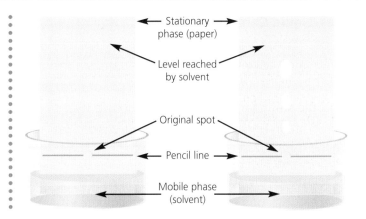

HT Different molecules in the sample mixture travel different distances according to how strongly they are attracted to the molecules in the stationary phase, in relation to their attraction to the solvent molecules.

Thin Layer Chromatography (TLC)

TLC is similar to paper chromatography. However, the stationary phase is a thin layer of adsorbent material (e.g. silica gel, alumina or cellulose) supported on a flat, unreactive surface (e.g. a glass, metal or plastic plate).

The advantages of TLC over paper chromatography include...

- faster runs
- more even movement of the mobile phase through the stationary phase
- a choice of different absorbent for the stationary phase (which can increase the attraction between molecules in the mixture and the stationary phase).

As a result, TLC usually produces better separations for a wider range of substances.

Some chromatograms have to be developed to show the presence of colourless substances:

- colourless spots can sometimes be viewed under ultraviolet (UV) light and then marked on the plate
- the chromatogram can be sprayed with a chemical that reacts with the spots to cause coloration.

R$_f$ Value

In paper and thin layer chromatography, the movement of a substance relative to the movement of the solvent front is known as the R$_f$ **value**:

$$R_f \text{ value} = \frac{\text{Distance travelled by substance}}{\text{Distance travelled by solvent}}$$

Example

The diagram below shows the distance travelled by a substance and the distance travelled by the solvent. Calculate the R$_f$ value.

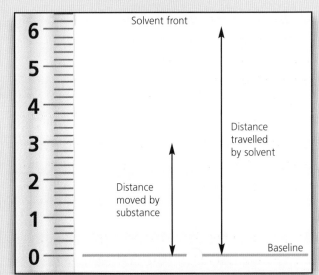

Use the formula:

$$R_f = \frac{\text{Distance travelled by substance}}{\text{Distance travelled by solvent}}$$

$$= \frac{3\text{cm}}{6\text{cm}} = \textbf{0.5cm}$$

Calculating the R$_f$ value can aid in the identification of unknown substances.

Scientific Detection

Gas–Liquid Chromatography

In gas–liquid chromatography, or simply gas chromatography (GC), the mobile phase is a carrier gas, usually an inert gas such as helium or nitrogen, and the stationary phase is a microscopic layer of liquid on an unreactive solid support, inside glass or metal tubing, called a **column**.

A sample of the substance to be analysed is injected into one end of the heated column where it vaporises. The carrier gas then carries it up the column where separation takes place.

GC has a greater separating power than TLC or paper chromatography, and can separate complex mixtures. It can produce quantitative data from very small samples of liquids, gases and volatile solids.

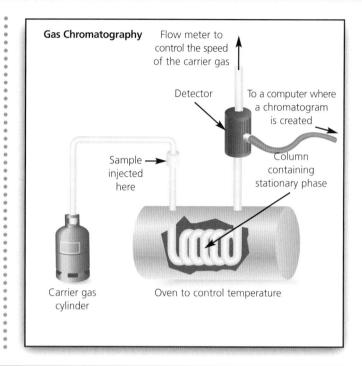

Gas Chromatography

Flow meter to control the speed of the carrier gas

Detector

To a computer where a chromatogram is created

Sample injected here

Column containing stationary phase

Carrier gas cylinder

Oven to control temperature

HT The size of each peak in the chromatogram produced by GC shows the relative amount of each chemical in the sample. For example, the chromatogram below shows six different compounds present in a sample.

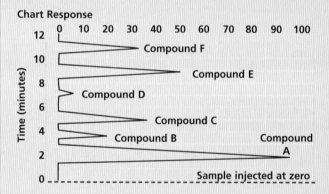

Chart Response

It can be seen that compound A is present in the largest amount and compound D in the smallest amount.

GC separates the components in a mixture because they have different solubilities in the stationary or mobile phases. Practical uses of GC include...

- detecting banned substances in blood and urine samples (random sampling of athletes)
- analysing the exact characteristics of oil or pesticide spills and matching them to samples from suspected sources to identify sources of pollution.

The time taken for each different substance to pass through the chromatographic system depends on its solubility and is called the **retention time**.

In gas–liquid chromatography, the retention time is the time taken from the sample being injected into the system to the substance being detected.

Tables of relative retention times show the retention times of different chemicals relative to the retention time of a specific compound.

Compound	Retention Time (minutes)
Methanol	2.24
A	2.08
B	2.24
C	3.01

The retention table above shows that Compound B could be methanol as the retention time is the same.

When choosing which chromatographic techniques to use, scientists will consider...

- the level of sensitivity required
- the separating power of each technique
- the limitations of detection for each technique.

Electrophoresis

Electrophoresis is a technique of separating different biological molecules, such as proteins. It can be used on small biological samples and for scientific detection, such as producing DNA profiles.

DNA profiling can be used...
- to help solve crimes by matching DNA found at the crime scene with DNA from a suspect or from the National DNA Database.
- in paternity testing to confirm a child's biological father. The pattern of DNA bands (a person's genetic code) is unique to each person, but some bands are shared by people who are related.

HT Electrophoresis separates components in a mixture as a result of the charges their particles carry.

The sample is absorbed onto damp paper, e.g. chromatography paper, or a gel. A charge of several thousand volts is then passed across the paper.

The positive particles move towards the negative electrode and the negative particles move towards the positive electrode.

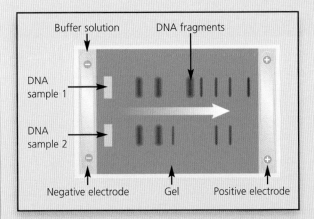

The separation and distance travelled depends on the size of the molecule and the number of charges:
- The smaller the molecule, the further it travels.
- The larger the charge, the further the molecule travels.

Colour Matching

Colour is widely used in analysis to give both qualitative and quantitative information.

An example of a qualitative test that relies on colour is the use of **litmus** to show whether a solution is acid or alkali. Red indicates an acid, and blue indicates an alkali.

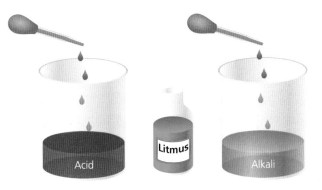

An example of a semi-quantitative test is the use of **universal indicator** to determine the pH of a solution.

The **pH scale** is a measure of the acidity or alkalinity of an aqueous solution across a 14-point scale. The colour scale provides a more accurate measure of pH levels than litmus, although it still requires a visual reading.

Colour Test Kits

Colour test kits are often used in medical diagnosis:
- Reagent strips (e.g. Clinistix®) are used by diabetics to check their glucose levels. The stick is dipped into a sample of urine for a set time and the colour of the strip is then compared to a colour chart, which can show the level of sugar in the urine.
- Pregnancy test kits are used to show whether or not a woman is pregnant. Different lines of colour are used to show whether the test is positive or negative.

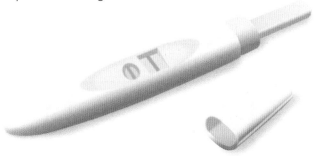

Scientific Detection

Colorimetry

A colorimeter is an instrument used to measure the intensity of a colour. It can be used to produce quantitative results.

Finding the Concentration of Coloured Chemicals

Before quantitative measurements can be made, a calibration graph is produced using a standard procedure and standard reference solutions (solutions of known concentration):

1. Pour a pure sample of the colourless solvent into a small test tube. Pass light through the solvent and set the colorimeter to zero.
2. Pass light through samples of standard coloured solutions and record the values on the meter. (This is the absorbance measurement.)
3. Plot the data (absorbance against concentration) to produce a calibration graph.
4. You can then use the calibration graph to work out the concentration of an unknown solution by passing light through it and comparing the meter value to the graph.

Example

The table below shows the concentration and absorbance of some standard reference solutions, and an unknown sample. Use the information to plot a graph and work out the concentration of Sample X.

Sample	Concentration (g/cm³)	Absorbance
1	0.080	0.09
2	0.16	0.19
3	0.24	0.28
4	0.32	0.37
5	0.34	0.22
6	0.4	0.46
X	Unknown	0.43

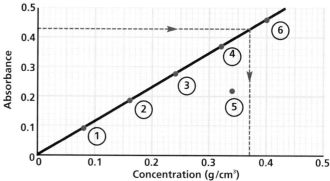

It can be seen from the graph that the concentration of Sample X is $0.37\,\text{g/cm}^3$

N.B. Sample 5 is an outlier and can therefore be ignored.

Colour Matching v Colorimetry

There are advantages and disadvantages to colour matching and colorimetry.

Colour matching is a quick, cheap technique that gives immediate results. However, it does not produce quantitative data.

Colorimetry does produce quantitative data, and gives greater sensitivity. It also produces an end point to a reaction. However, it is more expensive and it takes longer to calibrate and prepare samples.

HT Colour matching is used when only qualitative data is required. It is not very precise as it depends on how people see and interpret colour, i.e. different people can see colours as different shades. It is therefore limited in its use and cannot be used to determine concentrations of solutions.

In contrast, colorimetry provides quantitative data and can be used to determine a range of different concentrations. The sensitivity of the colorimeter will depend on the quality of the photocell in the meter.

The colorimeter monitors the light received by the photocell as either absorbance or percentage transmission. The darker the colour or more concentrated the solution, the higher the absorbance value.

Imaging

Images can be recorded in different ways. For example, a suspect seen at a crime scene could be recorded by any, or all, of the following methods:

1 A **written description**, e.g. the white man was tall, of medium build, with short black hair. He had tanned skin, a pointy nose, a small mouth and a scar on his left cheek. He was wearing black-rimmed glasses.

2 A **drawing**.

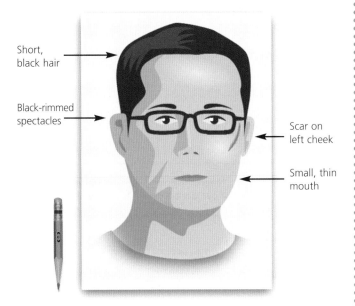

Short, black hair

Black-rimmed spectacles

Scar on left cheek

Small, thin mouth

3 A **photograph**.
4 **Video** – i.e. caught on CCTV camera.

Once an image of a potential suspect has been established, it can then be compared to a bank of similar images to look for an acceptable match. If a match is found, the suspect can be identified.

Taking Measurements

Measurements can be taken from an image or an object using a linear scale, such as a ruler. A measurement can be taken by estimating the reading between the graduations. For example, the ruler below shows a measurement of 6.05cm.

HT You need to ensure that accurate readings are taken, for example, if the end of a ruler is broken or worn, this could lead to systematic errors.

Calculating Measurements

Linear measurements can be used to calculate the area of various shapes:

- Rectangle: Area = Length x Height
- Square: Area = Length x Height
- Irregular shapes: Divide the shape up into squares. Measure the length of one square and calculate its area. Then multiply the area by the total number of squares.

Example

A rectangle has a length of 5.4cm and a height of 3.5cm. Calculate the area.

Area of rectangle = Length x Height
= 5.4 x 3.5 = **18.9cm^2**

HT A calculated area has a greater level of uncertainty than a single measured length because it is calculated from two or more measured lengths, each with a degree of uncertainty.

Scientific Detection

ⓗ A Vernier Scale

A Vernier scale is a small, moveable scale which gives more precise measurements. It is placed next to the main scale of a measuring instrument when a measurement lies between two marks on the same scale. For example, the Vernier scale below shows a measurement of 7.36mm.

Micrometer Screw Gauge

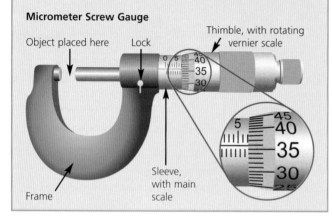

Light Microscopes

Microscopes are used to look at an image in more detail. Compound light microscopes do this by increasing the **magnification** and **resolution** of the image.

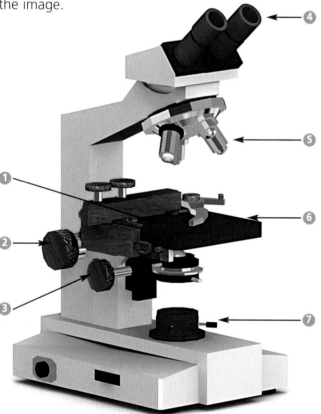

① **Stage** – where the slide is held.

② **Coarse focus** – used to move the objective lens up and down to bring the image into focus.

③ **Fine focus** – used to make slight adjustments, so that the detail of the image is clear.

④ **Eyepiece lens** – where you look into the microscope.

⑤ **Objective lens** – magnifies the specimen; there are usually three lenses, typically labelled x4, x10 and x40.

⑥ **Slide** – a rectangular piece of glass used to hold the specimen.

⑦ **Light source** – used to illuminate the specimen. (Some microscopes use a mirror instead of a light.)

Magnifying Power

Magnifying power can be calculated by the following equation:

$$\text{Magnifying power} = \text{Magnification of eyepiece lens} \times \text{Magnification of objective lens}$$

Example

A microscope with an eyepiece lens of magnification x10 is fitted with an objective lens of x40. Calculate the magnifying power.

$$\text{Magnifying power} = \text{Magnification of eyepiece lens} \times \text{Magnification of objective lens}$$

$$= 10 \times 40 = \mathbf{x400}$$

ⓗ The **resolving power** is the minimum distance by which two points must be separated in order for them to appear as separate points. A high resolving power microscope allows you to see details that are very closely spaced. The resolution of microscopes is limited by the nature of light.

The **depth of field** is the distance range in which a specimen is in acceptable focus. A light microscope has a very narrow depth of field which means that objects just above or below the image area appear blurred. The microscope has to be focused exactly on to the structure that is being examined.

Preparing Slides

Temporary light microscope slides are often prepared in the laboratory. The method depends on the sample.

Method 1: A Blood Sample

1. Place a small drop of blood on a clean slide.
2. Hold a second slide at an angle to the first one.
3. Pull the top slide back to touch the blood. The blood will start to spread.
4. Push the top slide away, causing a smear.
5. Cover the sample with a cover slip.

When preparing solid samples, e.g. slides of animal or plant cells, it is often necessary to stain the cellular material with a drop of iodine or methylene blue, before putting on the cover slip. The dye will make it easier to pick out the main features under the microscope.

Method 2: Plant Cells

1. Place the cell onto the microscope slide.
2. Use a mounted needle to lower a cover slip over the cells / tissue.
3. Stain the cells by placing a drop of coloured stain at the edge of the cover slip. Draw the stain under the cover slip using a piece of filter paper to remove the water.

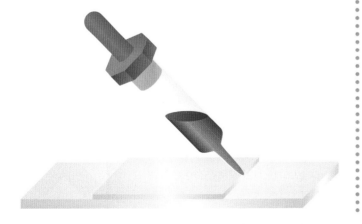

Electron Microscopes

An atom consists of a tiny positive nucleus surrounded by negative electrons. An electron microscope uses a beam of electrons (instead of a beam of light) and can be used to provide even greater detail than a light microscope.

An electron microscope shows greater detail because it has greater magnification. The resulting image is known as an **electron micrograph**.

> **HT** An electron microscope has a much greater depth of field than a light microscope. The electrons in the electron beam are so tiny that they can pick out parts of an object that are very close together. On an electron microscope, the **depth of field** refers to how much of the sample is in focus at the same time.

Electron microscope use is limited by the presentation and preparation of slides. They cannot be used to look at living specimens or biological materials because the microscope's process kills any live cells.

Some microscopes require very thin specimens that may need to be chemically treated to show up fine features, whilst others require biological samples to be treated with a thin layer of carbon or gold.

Comparing Microscopes

There are advantages and disadvantages to light and electron microscopes.

Light microscopes are cheap and portable, which means they can be taken into the field. Samples can be prepared quickly for immediate results, though the images are less detailed compared to electron microscopes because they have lower resolution and magnification powers.

Electron microscopes produce very detailed images due to high magnification and resolution. However, they are very expensive to buy and there are also high running costs. The microscopes are large and static and samples take a long time to prepare.

Harnessing Chemicals

The chemical industry uses a wide variety of raw materials to create many different products. This module looks at…

- the use of chemicals
- making soluble and insoluble salts
- how to make useful chemicals and mix formulations
- how to plan, control and cost chemical synthesis.

Chemicals

Chemicals are all around us. **Organic** chemicals all contain the element carbon and can either be obtained from **living** sources such as plants and animals, e.g. vegetable oil and wool, or from **non-living** sources (made from sources that once lived), e.g. crude oil, coal and natural gas.

Most **inorganic** chemicals do not contain carbon and are mainly obtained from sources that have **never lived** such as rocks, minerals and ores, e.g. iron and copper.

The Chemical Industry

The chemical industry synthesises chemicals on different scales according to their value:
- **Bulk** chemicals are made on a large scale, e.g. ammonia, sulfuric acid, sodium hydroxide and phosphoric acid.
- **Fine** chemicals are made on a small scale, e.g. drugs, food additives and fragrances.

New chemical products, such as medical drugs, are the result of an extensive programme of research and development. Products have to be thoroughly tested to ensure that they are effective and safe to use.

Health and Safety

Governments have a duty to protect people and the environment from any dangers that could occur as a result of procedures involving chemicals.

They impose strict regulations in order to control…
- the chemical processes
- the storage of chemicals
- the transportation of chemicals
- the research and development of chemicals.

In the UK, the Health and Safety Executive (HSE) is responsible for the regulation of risks to health and safety arising from the extraction, manufacture and use of chemicals.

All hazardous chemicals need to be labelled with these standard hazard symbols, as appropriate:

- **Toxic**
  These substances can kill when swallowed, breathed in or absorbed through the skin.

- **Oxidising**
  These substances provide oxygen, which allows other substances to burn more fiercely.

- **Harmful**
  These substances are similar to toxic substances, but they are less dangerous.

- **Highly flammable**
  These substances will catch fire easily. They pose a serious fire risk.

- **Corrosive**
  These substances attack living tissue, including eyes and skin, and can damage materials.

- **Irritant**
  These substances are not corrosive but they can cause the skin to blister.

Making Useful Chemicals

Equipment can be used to measure and transfer chemicals, carry out chemical reactions and conduct experiments.

When carrying out a chemical synthesis, chemists use a range of different techniques to ensure that the maximum yield of the product is produced by minimising the loss of chemicals during transfer, for example, ensuring that all chemicals are transferred from container to container and that nothing is spilt or lost.

The following equipment can be found in a research and development laboratory:

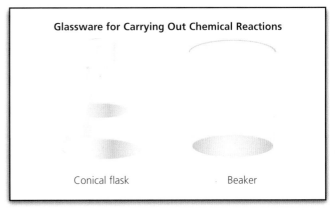

Glassware for Carrying Out Chemical Reactions

Conical flask   Beaker

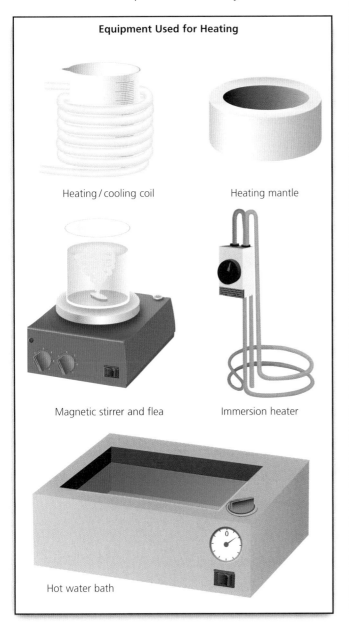

Equipment Used for Heating

Heating / cooling coil   Heating mantle

Magnetic stirrer and flea   Immersion heater

Hot water bath

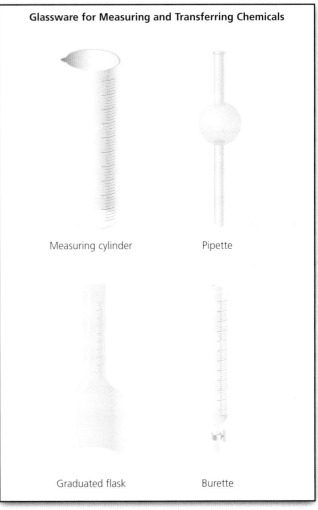

Glassware for Measuring and Transferring Chemicals

Measuring cylinder   Pipette

Graduated flask   Burette

Apparatus for Weighing

Balance

Harnessing Chemicals

Key

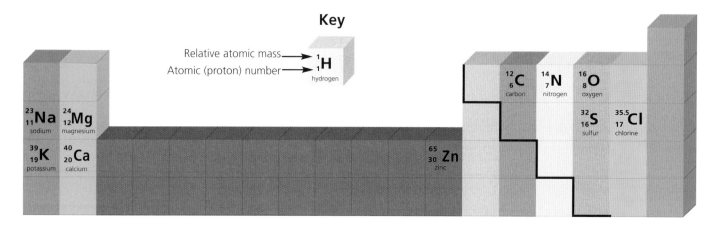

Chemicals

All the elements in the **Periodic Table** are represented by a different symbol. You need to learn the symbols for the chemicals shown in the Periodic Table above.

Chemical Formulae

When elements react they join together to form **compounds**. Chemical formulae are used to show the number of each atom present in a compound.

In chemical formulae, the position of the numbers tells you how many atoms of each element are present in a compound.

A small number that sits below the line (a subscript) multiplies only the symbol that comes immediately before it. For example, CO_2 (carbon dioxide), shows that there is 1 carbon atom and 2 oxygen atoms present in a molecule.

A number that is the same size as the letters, multiplies all the symbols that come after it. For example, $2H_2SO_4$ (sulfuric acid), shows that there are 2 molecules of sulfuric acid. In each molecule there are 2 hydrogen atoms, 1 sulfur atom and 4 oxygen atoms.

If there is a bracket around two or more symbols, then all the atoms within the bracket are multiplied by the number outside the bracket. For example, $Mg(OH)_2$ (magnesium hydroxide), shows that there is 1 magnesium atom, 2 oxygen atoms and 2 hydrogen atoms.

Word equations are used to represent chemical reactions. For example, carbon and oxygen react to produce carbon dioxide. The word equation is as follows:

carbon + oxygen ⟶ carbon dioxide

Balanced symbol equations can also be used to represent reactions. The equation for the reaction between carbon and oxygen would be:

$$C_{(s)} + O_{2(g)} \longrightarrow CO_{2(g)}$$

Relative Formula Mass

The relative formula mass, M_r, of a compound is the sum of the relative atomic masses of all its elements.

To calculate M_r, we need to know the formula of the compound and the relative atomic mass (A_r) of each of the atoms involved. For example...

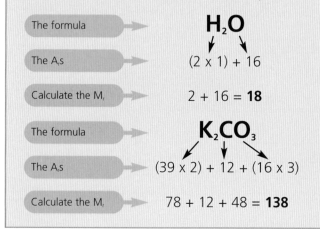

The formula	H_2O
The A_rs	$(2 \times 1) + 16$
Calculate the M_r	$2 + 16 = \mathbf{18}$
The formula	K_2CO_3
The A_rs	$(39 \times 2) + 12 + (16 \times 3)$
Calculate the M_r	$78 + 12 + 48 = \mathbf{138}$

Harnessing Chemicals

Formulae

You need to know the following formulae for oxides, hydroxides and salts:

Chemical	Formula
calcium oxide	CaO
magnesium oxide	MgO
zinc oxide	ZnO
calcium hydroxide	$Ca(OH)_2$
magnesium hydroxide	$Mg(OH)_2$
potassium hydroxide	KOH
sodium hydroxide	NaOH
calcium carbonate	$CaCO_3$
magnesium carbonate	$MgCO_3$
sodium carbonate	Na_2CO_3
zinc carbonate	$ZnCO_3$
calcium chloride	$CaCl_2$
potassium chloride	KCl
sodium chloride	NaCl
potassium nitrate	KNO_3
sodium nitrate	$NaNO_3$
magnesium sulfate	$MgSO_4$
sodium sulfate	Na_2SO_4
zinc sulfate	$ZnSO_4$
carbon dioxide	CO_2
water	H_2O

Acids

The **pH scale** is a measure of the acidity or alkalinity of an aqueous solution, across a 14-point scale. **Acids** are substances that have a pH less than 7. Common acids include hydrochloric acid (HCl), sulfuric acid (H_2SO_4) and nitric acid (HNO_3).

Below are some characteristic reactions of acids:

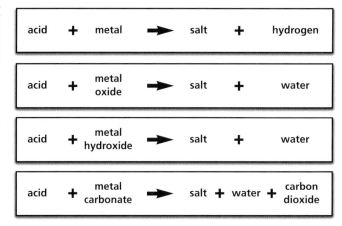

N.B. A salt is a substance that is formed as a result of a neutralisation reaction.

Alkalis

Alkalis are bases (the oxides and hydroxides of metals) which dissolve in water and produce solutions that have a pH above 7. They neutralise acids to form **salts**.

Preparation of Salts

Different methods can be used for making a salt depending on its properties. You will need to know the terms used below.

A **soluble** chemical is a **solute** (solid) which will dissolve in a **solvent** (liquid) to make a **solution**. An **insoluble** chemical will not dissolve in a solvent.

An **aqueous** solution is made when a solute dissolves in the solvent water. A **non-aqueous** solution is made when a solute dissolves in any solvent except for water, e.g. an organic hydrocarbon solvent.

Precipitation is the formation of a **precipitate** (insoluble solid) when two solutions are mixed.

Filtration is the method of separating solid particles from a liquid by passing the mixture through a porous material. The **filtrate** is the clear liquid which passes through the filter during filtration.

An **insoluble residue** is any insoluble substance left behind after a filtration or other similar chemical process.

Harnessing Chemicals

Making Insoluble Salts

An insoluble salt is made by mixing together two solutions, using the following method:

1 Measure out known amounts of two solutions into separate measuring beakers. Pour the solutions into a beaker and mix with a glass rod. A precipitate will form.

2 Fold some filter paper and place it in a funnel. Place the funnel in a conical flask. Pour the mixture into the filter funnel; the precipitate will be separated by filtration.

3 Pour some distilled water into the beaker to help remove the final bits of chemical. Pour the water and chemicals onto the filter paper. (This will also remove any unreacted chemicals sticking to the insoluble residue.)

4 Remove the precipitate and dry in a desiccator or an oven. An insoluble salt will now form.

Examples

Lead iodide is made by mixing solutions of potassium iodide and lead nitrate:

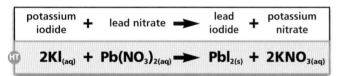

| potassium iodide | + | lead nitrate | ➡ | lead iodide | + | potassium nitrate |

HT $2KI_{(aq)} + Pb(NO_3)_{2(aq)} \rightarrow PbI_{2(s)} + 2KNO_{3(aq)}$

Silver chloride is made by mixing solutions of silver nitrate and sodium chloride:

| sodium chloride | + | silver nitrate | ➡ | silver chloride | + | sodium nitrate |

HT $NaCl_{(aq)} + AgNO_{3(aq)} \rightarrow AgCl_{(s)} + NaNO_{3(aq)}$

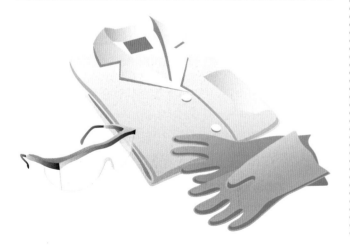

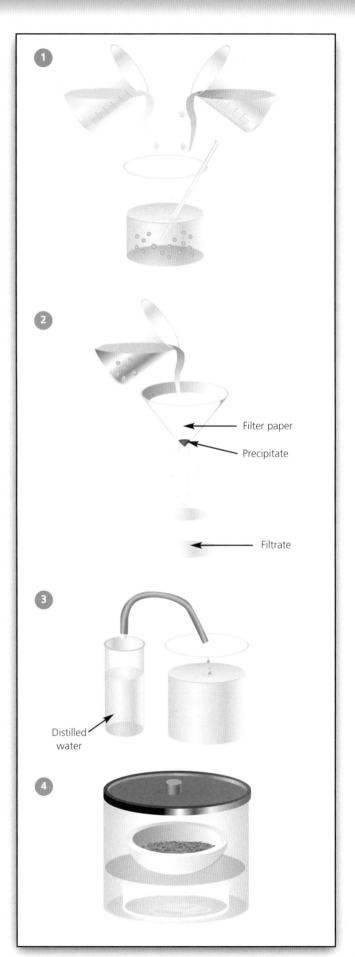

Filter paper

Precipitate

Filtrate

Distilled water

Making Soluble Salts

There are two methods for making soluble salts:

Method 1
Soluble salts can be made when an insoluble metal, a metal oxide, a metal hydroxide or a metal carbonate reacts with a soluble acid in solution.

This method involves **evaporation** (slowly heating a product to remove water) and **crystallisation** (the formation of a solid during cooling). Any matter left behind by the reaction is called the **residue**.

1. Measure out a known amount of acid in a measuring cylinder and pour it into a beaker. Add the solid until no further reactions take place, i.e. no more gas is given off. (Warming up the acid will increase the rate of reaction.)
2. Fold some filter paper and place it in a funnel. Place the funnel in a conical flask and filter the solution to remove the excess solid residue.
3. Pour the filtrate into a basin and evaporate slowly. The solution will slowly form crystals that will cling to the end of a cold glass rod. Leave to cool and crystallise. (The size of the crystals often depends on the rate of evaporation of the water. The slower the rate of evaporation, the larger the crystals formed.)
4. Filter the crystals to separate them from any solution left behind.
5. Wash the crystals with distilled water.
6. Dry the crystals in a desiccator or oven.

Examples

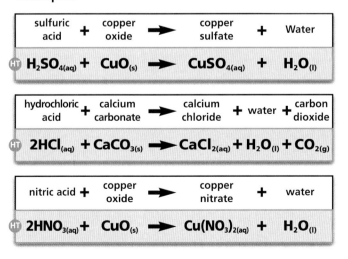

| sulfuric acid | + | copper oxide | → | copper sulfate | + | Water |

$H_2SO_{4(aq)} + CuO_{(s)} \rightarrow CuSO_{4(aq)} + H_2O_{(l)}$

| hydrochloric acid | + | calcium carbonate | → | calcium chloride | + water + | carbon dioxide |

$2HCl_{(aq)} + CaCO_{3(s)} \rightarrow CaCl_{2(aq)} + H_2O_{(l)} + CO_{2(g)}$

| nitric acid | + | copper oxide | → | copper nitrate | + | water |

$2HNO_{3(aq)} + CuO_{(s)} \rightarrow Cu(NO_3)_{2(aq)} + H_2O_{(l)}$

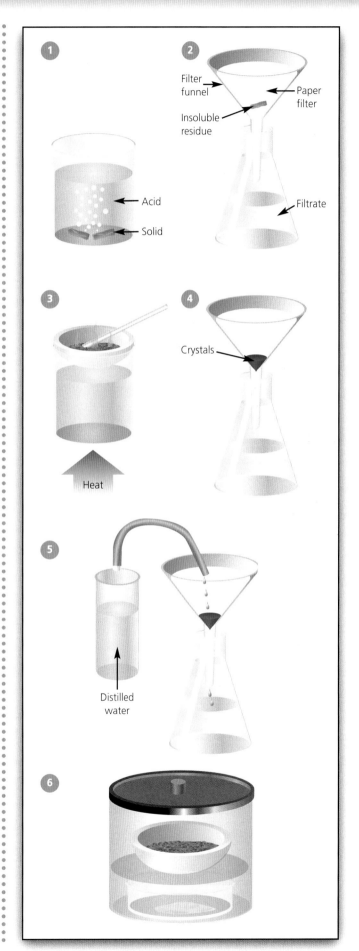

Harnessing Chemicals

Making Soluble Salts (cont.)

Method 2 – Titration

Soluble salts can also be made by reacting two solutions and crystallising a solid product. A complete reaction can be monitored when neutralising an acid with an alkali.

1. Fill a burette with an alkali, such as sodium hydroxide.
2. Pipette a known amount of acid, e.g. 25cm³ into a conical flask. Add a few drops of indicator such as phenolphthalein to the conical flask (this will stay colourless unless alkali is present). Place the flask on a white tile.
3. Add the alkali from the burette to the flask. Swirl the flask to ensure it mixes well. Near the end of the reaction, the indicator will start to turn pink. Keep swirling and adding the alkali until all the indicator is completely pink, showing that the acid has been neutralised. Record the volume of alkali added by subtracting the amount in the burette at the end of the reaction from the starting value.
4. Filter the solution through activated charcoal (charcoal treated with oxygen) to remove the indicator.
5. Pour the filtrate into an evaporation basin and evaporate it. Leave it to cool and crystallise.
6. Filter the crystals from any solution left behind.
7. Wash the crystals with distilled water and dry in a desiccator or oven.

N.B. If a pH meter is used in step 2 instead of an indicator, then in step 3 the alkali is added until pH 7 is recorded by the pH meter, and activated charcoal is not needed in step 4.

Examples

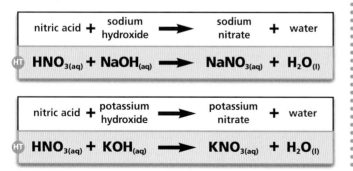

| nitric acid | + | sodium hydroxide | → | sodium nitrate | + | water |

HT $HNO_{3(aq)} + NaOH_{(aq)} \longrightarrow NaNO_{3(aq)} + H_2O_{(l)}$

| nitric acid | + | potassium hydroxide | → | potassium nitrate | + | water |

HT $HNO_{3(aq)} + KOH_{(aq)} \longrightarrow KNO_{3(aq)} + H_2O_{(l)}$

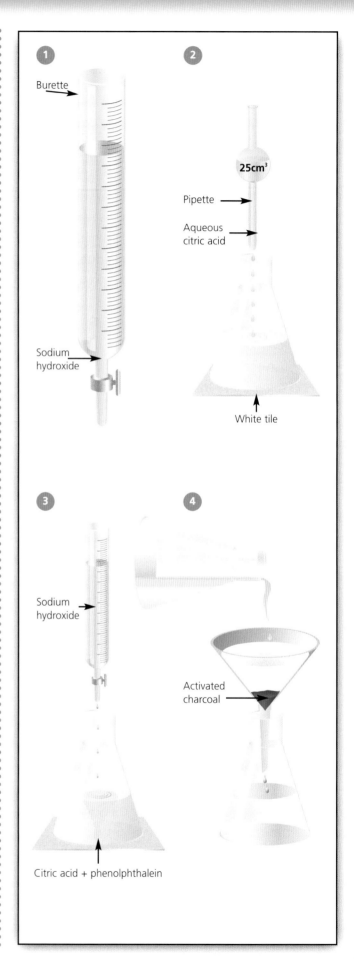

1 Burette

Sodium hydroxide

2 25cm³

Pipette

Aqueous citric acid

White tile

3 Sodium hydroxide

Citric acid + phenolphthalein

4 Activated charcoal

Harnessing Chemicals

Organic Compounds

All organic compounds contain carbon atoms. However, **hydrocarbons** contain only carbon and hydrogen atoms. Other organic compounds such as **alcohols** and **carboxylic acids** contain carbon, hydrogen and some oxygen atoms. The **functional group** of the molecule tells us whether the molecule is a hydrocarbon, an alcohol or a carboxylic acid. (See table at foot of page).

N.B. You must be able to recognise these compounds from their chemical formulae.

Esters

Esters are organic molecules made by reacting an alcohol and a carboxylic acid in the presence of a strong acidic catalyst, e.g. sulfuric acid. They are reacted by **reflux** (continuous heating) and **distillation** (the process of evaporating a liquid and then condensing the vapour). The **distillate** is the liquid produced during distillation. After the reaction has occurred the ester is removed by distillation and the distillate is collected in a clean flask.

HT The reaction between an alcohol and carboxylic acid to make ester is as follows:

carboxylic acid + alcohol ⟶ ester + water

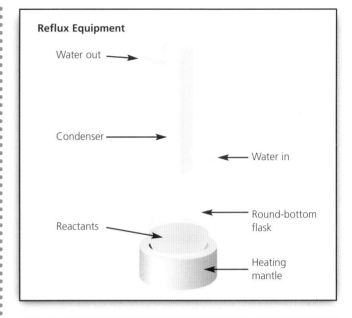

Reflux Equipment

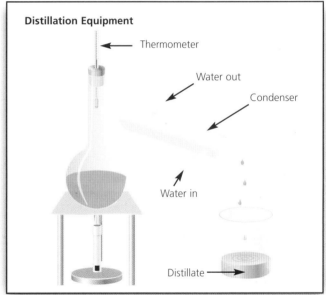

Distillation Equipment

	Hydrocarbon (Alkane)	Hydrocarbon (Alkene)	Alcohol		Carboxylic Acid	
Functional Group	None	None	-OH		-COOH	
Example of Chemical	methane	propene	ethanol	propanol	ethanoic acid	propanoic acid
Chemical Formula	CH_4	C_3H_6	C_2H_5OH	C_3H_7OH	CH_3CO_2H	$C_2H_5CO_2H$
Displayed Formula						

Rates of Reactions

The **rate of a chemical reaction** is the amount of reaction that takes place in a given unit of time.

Chemical reactions only occur when the reacting particles collide with each other with sufficient energy to react. Reactions can occur at different speeds.

The rate of a chemical reaction can be found in three different ways:

1 **Weighing the reaction mixture**

If one of the products is a gas, the mass of the mixture will decrease as the gas is produced, so the reaction mixture can be weighed at timed intervals in order to find the reaction rate.

2 **Measuring the volume of gas produced**

If one of the products is a gas, a gas syringe can be used to collect and measure the total volume of gas produced at timed intervals.

3 **Observing the formation of a precipitate**

This can be done by…

- watching a cross (on a piece of paper placed at the bottom of the jar containing the reaction) to see when it is no longer visible
- measuring the formation of a precipitate or a colour change using a light sensor.

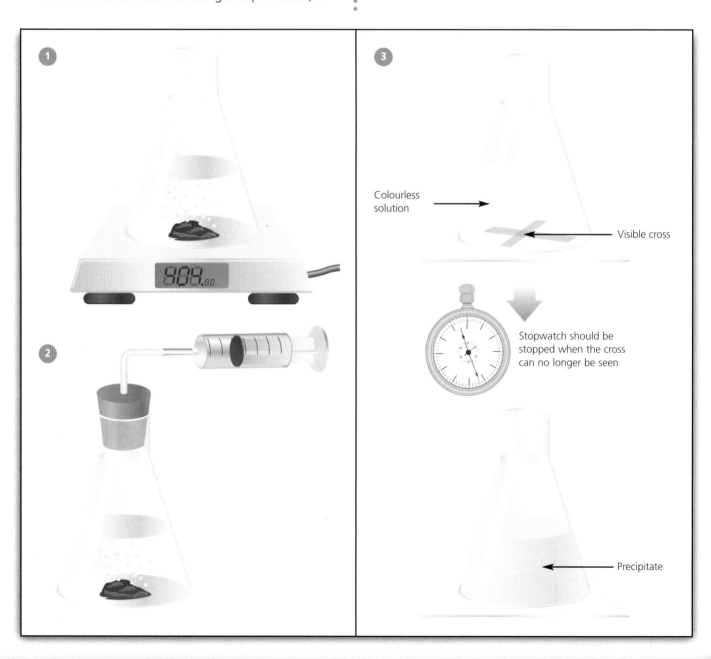

Colourless solution

Visible cross

Stopwatch should be stopped when the cross can no longer be seen

Precipitate

Changing the Rate of the Reaction

There are three factors which affect the rate of a reaction:

1. The temperature of the reaction mixture.
2. The concentration of a solution of the soluble chemical.
3. The particle size of an insoluble chemical.

Temperature of the Reactants

Low Temperature

In a cold reaction mixture, the particles move quite slowly. They collide less often, with less energy, so fewer collisions will be successful.

High Temperature

In a hot reaction mixture, the particles move more quickly. They collide more often, with greater energy, so many more collisions will be successful.

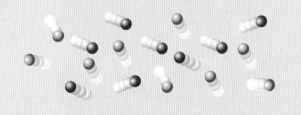

Concentration of the Dissolved Reactants

Low Concentration

In a low-concentration reaction, the particles are spread out. The particles collide with each other less often, resulting in fewer successful collisions.

High Concentration

In a high-concentration reaction, the particles are crowded close together. The particles therefore collide with each other more often, resulting in many more successful collisions.

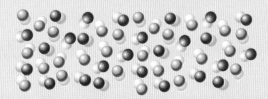

Surface Area of Solid Reactants

Large Particles

Large particles (e.g. granulated solids) have a small surface area in relation to their volume, so fewer particles are exposed and available for collisions. This means fewer collisions and a slower reaction.

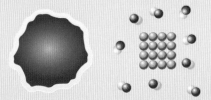

Small Particles

Small particles (e.g. powdered solids) have a large surface area in relation to their volume, so more particles are exposed and available for collisions. This means more collisions and a faster reaction.

Harnessing Chemicals

Chemical Synthesis

It is important to choose the most efficient method when preparing a chemical. Some chemicals can be made in a single-step process whilst others require many stages. In an industrial or commercial synthesis, factors to consider include the energy requirements, yields, costs, and disposal or recycling of side products.

Energy Requirements

Chemical reactions can be...

- **exothermic** – they give out energy in the form of heat, light or sound. In efficient systems, the 'waste' heat energy from exothermic reactions can be recycled and used to heat other areas of the reaction plant. If the heat energy is not recycled, it is lost to the surroundings.
- **endothermic** – they take in heat energy from the surroundings.

In order to reduce production costs and the emission of pollutant gases, reaction plants need to manage their energy usage efficiently.

Yield

The amount of product made in a chemical reaction is known as the **yield**. Calculating the yield shows how efficient a reaction has been.

The percentage yield is calculated by comparing the amount of product made (**actual yield**) to the amount of product expected to be made if the reaction goes to completion (**theoretical yield**).

$$\text{Percentage yield} = \frac{\text{Actual yield}}{\text{Theoretical yield}} \times 100$$

Example

An experiment was undertaken to make copper sulfate crystals. It was expected that 16.3g copper sulfate crystals would be produced, but at the end of the experiment the crystals weighed in at 15.2g. Calculate the percentage yield.

$$\text{Percentage yield} = \frac{15.2}{16.3} \times 100 = \textbf{93.3\%}$$

Calculating Theoretical Yield

The theoretical yield can be calculated when the chemical equation and the relative formula masses (M_r) are known.

Example

Calculate the theoretical yield of copper sulfate produced by 10g sulfuric acid.

Equation: $CuO + H_2SO_4 = CuSO_4 + H_2O$

$$M_r : \quad 80 + 98 = 160 + 18$$

The amount of CuO added is in excess and can be ignored, and all the acid is used up in the reaction.

The ratio of mass of reactant to mass of product is 98 : 160

When 98g acid is used, 160g copper sulfate is produced. Therefore, when 1g acid is used, $\frac{160}{98}$g copper sulfate is produced.

Therefore, 10g acid produces:

$$\frac{160}{98} \times 10 = \textbf{16.3g} \text{ copper sulfate.}$$

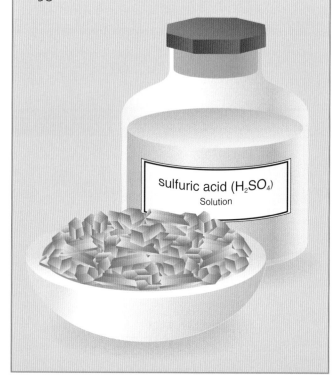

Sulfuric acid (H_2SO_4)
Solution

Purity and Cost of Chemicals

Chemical substances are available in different levels of purity. The purity of the chemical required depends on the eventual use of the manufactured product.

Technical grade chemicals are not very pure, and are, therefore, the cheapest. These chemicals may be used during preliminary experiments or where purity is not important (when the chemical is in excess).

Laboratory grade chemicals are purer than technical grade chemicals and are therefore more expensive. These chemicals are often used to manufacture products on a larger scale. The purity of the reactants will affect the overall yield of the product.

Analytical grade chemicals are very pure and therefore very expensive. These chemicals are used when purity is crucial, (e.g. during analytical experiments which detect very low concentrations of other chemicals) and to manufacture products which require a very high level of purity (e.g. medicines).

For example, the cost of different grades of magnesium sulfate are shown in the table below.

Chemical Type	Cost per 1kg
Technical	£1.20
Laboratory	£3.60
Analytical	£22.60

When working out the cost of making a product, the purity of the reactants must be taken into account.

Industrial Scale Chemicals

There are several issues that must be considered when a laboratory preparation is scaled up to an industrial plan:
- type of vessel
- method of transferring liquids
- method of mixing
- method of heating or cooling
- method for separating the product
- method for removing impurities.

Chemicals can be produced by a **batch** or a **continuous** process.

In a batch process, a specific amount of a product is made at any time. It may be left to react in the same reaction vessel for several days or weeks.

Advantages
- Maintenance can be carried out on some vessels while others are being used, so production continues.
- If a reactant is contaminated it will only affect one batch.

Disadvantages
- Production is slower and less efficient.
- Batches may be slightly different from each other.
- Because a vessel could be used for different reactions, the product could become contaminated and would, therefore, be less pure.

In a continuous process, reactants are continuously fed into the system and move through all the different steps of processing. The product comes out continuously at the other end.

Advantages
- Production is quick, efficient and cost-effective as the plant is running 24 hours a day.
- Product is likely to be 100% pure.

Disadvantages
- Maintenance is expensive as all production is lost when the plant is shut down.
- If a reactant is contaminated it will affect the whole production.

Harnessing Chemicals

Sustainable Development

The chemical industry carries out research and development to ensure that its processes are **sustainable**, i.e. meet the needs of present generations without compromising future generations. The industry is looking for ways to…

- use renewable resources rather than relying on non-renewable resources
- use less energy
- maximise yields
- produce less waste
- use or recycle waste products.

A **catalyst** is a substance which changes the rate of a chemical reaction whilst remaining chemically unchanged itself. A large reaction can, therefore, be created using only a small amount of energy and, as the catalyst remains unchanged, it can be used over and over again. This makes a chemical process more sustainable.

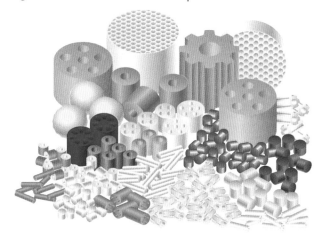

Quality Control

The effectiveness of chemicals, both pure and formulation, is tested as part of the quality-control process. Tests are undertaken on product formulations to ensure…

- quality assurance
- consumer protection
- conformity to national and international standards.

National and international standards for testing are needed to ensure that a certain level of quality of chemicals is reached as different countries may have different tests and standards.

Emulsions

An **emulsion** consists of one liquid finely dispersed in another liquid, e.g. mayonnaise (oil in water) and liquid soaps.

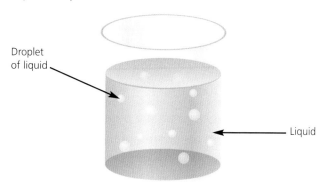

Droplet of liquid

Liquid

When making an emulsion from two liquids that do not usually mix, **emulsifying agents** can be used to stop them from separating.

A **suspension** consists of a solid dispersed in a liquid, e.g. water-based ink or paint.

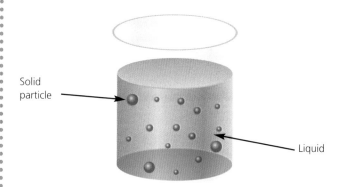

Solid particle

Liquid

Solid Mixtures

An **alloy** is a mixture of two or more solid metals or a mixture of a metal and a non-metal where the metal is the major component. Alloys are very useful materials as it is possible to make them with specific properties. For example:

- Coins are made from copper alloys, e.g. 2p coins are 97% copper, 2.5% zinc and 0.5% tin; 50p coins are 75% copper and 25% nickel.
- Aircraft bodyworks and window frames are made from duralumin, which is an alloy of aluminium and copper.
- Cutlery is made from stainless steel, an alloy of iron that contains 20% chromium and 10% nickel.

Harnessing Chemicals

Formulations and Effectiveness

Mixing ingredients according to a fixed formula is called **formulation**. The following method details how a 100cm³ copper sulfate solution is made using 5g of copper sulfate, to a concentration of 0.05g/cm³.

1. Weigh out 5g copper sulfate in a beaker.
2. Transfer the solid copper sulfate into a volumetric flask using a short-stem funnel. Wash the funnel and beaker with distilled water. Pour the washings into the volumetric flask (this will ensure that all of the solid has been transferred).
3. Add distilled water to the flask until it is about three-quarters full. Place the stopper in the top and gently shake until all the solid is dissolved.
4. Place the flask on a level surface and fill it up with water until the level of solution reaches the 100cm³ mark (see diagram opposite).

When preparing a solution, make sure that you read the concentration units carefully. The concentration can be expressed in…

- grams per litre (g/litre)
- grams per cubic centimetre (g/cm³)

N.B. 1 litre = 1000ml; 1ml = 1cm³.

When the concentration and volume of a solution is known you can calculate the mass of a solute using the following formula:

$$\text{Mass (g)} = \frac{\text{Concentration}}{\text{(g/litre or g/cm}^3\text{)}} \times \frac{\text{Volume}}{\text{(litre or cm}^3\text{)}}$$

Example 1

A 80cm³ solution of copper sulfate is prepared at a concentration of 45g/litre. Calculate the mass.

$$\text{Mass} = 45\text{g/litre} \times \frac{80\text{cm}^3}{1000}$$

to convert cm³ to litres divide by 1000

$$= \textbf{3.6g}$$

Example 2

Calculate the mass of a solute if the concentration of a formulation is 35g/litre and the volume is 3 litres.

$$\text{Mass} = 35\text{g/litre} \times 3 \text{ litres}$$

$$= \textbf{105g}$$

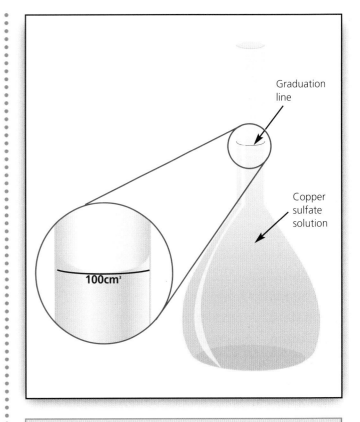

Graduation line

Copper sulfate solution

100cm³

(HT) Parts per million (ppm) can also be used to express concentration. When calculating the mass of a solution, we make the assumption that the density of the solution is the same as the density of water:

$$\text{Density} = \frac{\text{Mass}}{\text{Volume}}$$

A density of 1g/cm³ means that 1g of water has a volume of 1cm³

So, in a copper sulfate solution of concentration 300ppm, there are 300 parts of copper sulfate for every 999 700 parts of water, or 300g of copper sulfate in 999 700g of water.

To calculate the mass of copper sulfate that would need to be dissolved in a volume of 100cm³ of water to give a concentration of 300ppm, you can use ratios:

$$\frac{300}{999\,700} = \frac{\text{Mass of copper sulfate}}{100}$$

$$\text{Mass of copper sulfate} = \frac{300 \times 100}{999\,700} = \textbf{0.03g}$$

Glossary

Acid – a compound with a pH value less than 7

Alkali – a compound with a pH value greater than 7

Aqueous solution – a solution made when a solute dissolves in water

Bulk chemicals – chemicals produced on a large scale

Catalyst – a substance which changes the rate of a chemical reaction whilst remaining chemically unchanged itself

Chromatography – a technique used to separate unknown mixtures for analysis

Colorimeter – an instrument used to measure the intensity of a colour

Crystallisation – the formation of solid crystals from a solution

Distillate – the product of distillation

Distillation – the process of evaporation followed by condensation to produce a pure substance

Electron microscope – an instrument which uses a beam of electrons to magnify an object

Electrophoresis – a process which separates charged particles and can be used to identify small biological samples

Emulsion – a substance that contains one liquid finely dispersed in another liquid

Endothermic reaction – a reaction which absorbs energy from the surroundings

Evaporation – the process of heating a substance in order to remove the moisture by vaporisation

Exothermic reaction – a reaction which gives out energy to the surroundings

Filtrate – the clear liquid produced during filtration

Filtration – separating solid particles from a liquid

Fine chemicals – produced on a small scale

Inorganic – a compound that does not contain carbon

Insoluble – a substance that does not dissolve in a solvent

Insoluble residue – the insoluble substance left behind by a chemical reaction

Light microscope – an instrument which uses a beam of light to magnify an object

Mobile phase – the solvent that carries chemicals from a sample through the stationary phase during chromatography

Neutralisation – the reaction between an acid and a base which forms a neutral solution of pH 7

Non-aqueous solution – a solution made when a solute dissolves in a solvent other than water

Organic – a compound that contains carbon

Organic chemistry – the study of chemicals from plants and animals, including the study of synthetic compounds such as polymers, dyes and drugs

Precipitate – an insoluble solid formed during a precipitation process

Precipitation – the formation of an insoluble solid when two solutions containing ions are mixed together

Reflux – a process of continuous heating without the loss of volatile substances

Residue – the substance that remains after evaporation, distillation, filtration or a similar process

Salt – the product of a chemical reaction between a base and an acid

Stationary phase – the medium through which the mobile phase travels in chromatography

Suspension – a solid dispersed in a liquid

Titration – a method used to measure how much of one solution is needed to react exactly with another of known volume

Universal indicator – mixture of pH indicators, used to measure the acidity or alkalinity of a solution

Yield – the amount of product obtained from a reaction

(HT) **Depth of field** – the distance range from specimen to lens in which a specimen is in acceptable focus

Relative formula mass (M_r) – the sum of the atomic masses of all atoms in a molecule

Resolving power – the minimum distance by which two points need to be separated in order for them to appear as separate points

R_f value – the movement of a substance relative to the movement of the solvent front

Retention – the time taken for substances to pass through a chromatographic system

Vernier scale – a small moveable scale, used in conjunction with a linear scale, to take more accurate measurements

Module Ap5

Communication is an essential part of our lives. This module looks at...

- electronic circuits
- communication systems
- electronic systems
- radio waves
- sending information, signals and images.

Electronic Circuits

Standard circuit symbols are used when drawing electronic circuits. You need to know the circuit symbols for the following components:

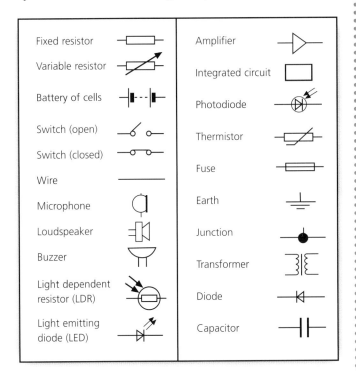

Fixed resistor	Amplifier
Variable resistor	Integrated circuit
Battery of cells	Photodiode
Switch (open)	Thermistor
Switch (closed)	Fuse
Wire	Earth
Microphone	Junction
Loudspeaker	Transformer
Buzzer	Diode
Light dependent resistor (LDR)	Capacitor
Light emitting diode (LED)	

Series and Parallel Circuits

In a series circuit all components are connected one after another in a single loop going from one terminal of the battery to another.

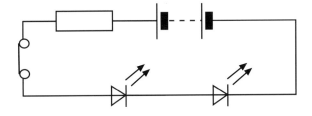

In a parallel circuit the components are connected in separate loops going from one terminal of the battery to another.

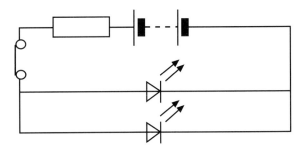

HT In a series circuit the voltages across each component add up to the supply voltage.

Currents at a Junction

In a parallel circuit the current splits or joins up at junctions.

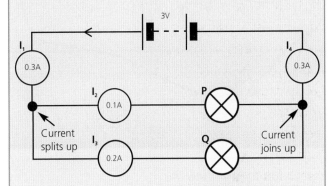

The amount of current which passes through a component depends on the resistance of the component; the greater the resistance, the smaller the current.

In the circuit above, Bulb Q has half the resistance of Bulb P, so twice as much current flows through it.

The current is smallest through the component with the largest resistance.

The total current running from (and back to) the battery is equal to the sum of the current through each of the parallel components, i.e. $I_1 = I_2 + I_3 = I_4$. Therefore, for the circuit above 0.3A = 0.1A + 0.2A = 0.3A.

Communications

Current

Resistance, which is measured in ohms (Ω), is a measure of how hard it is for a current to pass through a component at a particular potential difference or voltage.

Current can be calculated by the following formula:

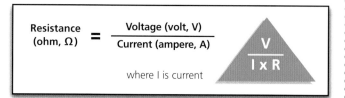

Resistance (ohm, Ω) $=$ $\dfrac{\text{Voltage (volt, V)}}{\text{Current (ampere, A)}}$

where I is current

$$\dfrac{V}{I \times R}$$

Example

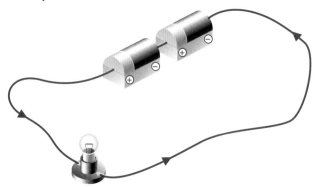

The circuit above has a resistance of 2Ω and a voltage of 6V. What is the current?

Rearrange the formula:

$$\text{Current} = \dfrac{\text{Voltage}}{\text{Resistance}}$$

$$= \dfrac{6V}{2\Omega}$$

$$= \textbf{3A}$$

Power

When charge flows through a component, energy is transferred to the component. Power, measured in watts (W), is a measure of how much energy is transferred by a device every second, i.e. the rate of energy transfer.

Power can be calculated using the following formula:

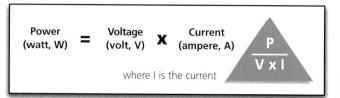

Power (watt, W) $=$ Voltage (volt, V) $\times$ Current (ampere, A)

where I is the current

$$\dfrac{P}{V \times I}$$

Example

An iron works at a current of 10A and a voltage of 220V. What is the heating power of the iron?

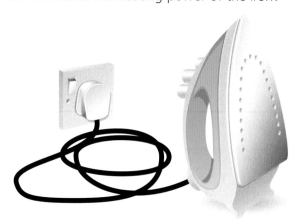

Power $=$ Voltage x Current

$= 10V \times 220A$

$= \textbf{2200W}$

All electrical components and devices have a maximum rating for power, voltage and current.

Exceeding this rating could cause the component to break, i.e. if a bulb is connected to a power supply that is too large, too much current could flow which would melt the filament in the bulb causing it to 'blow'.

> **HT** Many electronic components are designed to work at very low currents, so it is easy for the power supply to overload the component. To prevent this happening, a large resistor is placed in series with the component. Because they are in series, the total resistance is the resistance of the component **plus** the resistance of the resistor. The large total resistance, therefore, results in a smaller current flowing.

Mains or Battery

Many communication systems can be either **mains** or **battery operated**. The mains supply is suitable for a reliable high-power system, for example a radio transmitter, whilst battery power can be used for portable receivers in locations where there is no mains supply.

Communications

Electronic Systems

Basic electronic systems have **input**, **output** and **processor** devices which all have different functions. Input devices collect data, and output devices convert the processed signal into a format the user can understand, e.g. sound or light.

> Processor devices manipulate the signal / information in some way, e.g. encryption, compression, etc.

Details of electronic systems can be described using a circuit diagram that shows the details of individual components. For example, a simple circuit diagram for the output stage of a system could include a switch, variable resistor, battery and loudspeaker as shown in the diagram below.

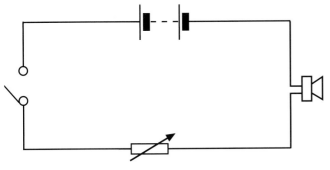

Electronic systems can also be represented by a connected set of blocks where each block represents a process, and arrows join blocks to show the flow of information. So, for the example above, a single block labelled 'loudspeaker' would be used:

The simplest communication systems can be represented with just three blocks illustrating the three stages of the system.

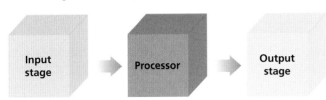

Examples

Telephone

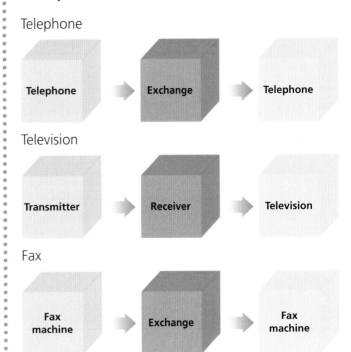

Television

Fax

Examples of simple signalling systems, and a description of each part are shown below:

Scanning and printing images:

	Device	Function
Input	Scanner	Converts image into electrical signal.
Processor	CPU (central processing unit)	Processes electrical signal into a format recognisable by the printer.
Output	Printer	Converts electrical signal into an image.

Telephone conversations:

	Device	Function
Input	Telephone	Converts sound into an electrical signal.
Processor	Exchange transmitter	Passes the signal between the telephones.
Output	Telephone	Converts electrical signal into sound.

Communications

Analogue Signals

Naturally occurring signals, e.g. light and sound, are analogue signals and can take any value.

An analogue signal gives a true representation of the signal and it can be carried by simple transmitters and receivers.

However, this type of signal is difficult to compress and encrypt and, during compression, the signal becomes weaker and picks up noise. When the signal is amplified at the receiver, the noise is difficult to remove and is also amplified. Information can, therefore, become distorted and degraded during transmission.

Digital Signals

An analogue signal can be converted into a digital format where it is limited to discrete values (0s and 1s).

Digital signals can be manipulated and transferred with little loss of quality as any interference can be easily removed. Digital signals can carry more information per second than analogue signals, so they are more versatile and can be used in a range of digital devices.

However, not all values are possible which leads to distortion, and complex circuitry is needed at the transmitter and receiver to convert to, and from, analogue. This increases the cost of equipment.

> **HT** A signal-to-noise ratio is the amount of a given transmitted signal compared with the background noise during transmission. Digital signals maintain a high signal-to-noise ratio which means that they can be transmitted with little loss of quality.

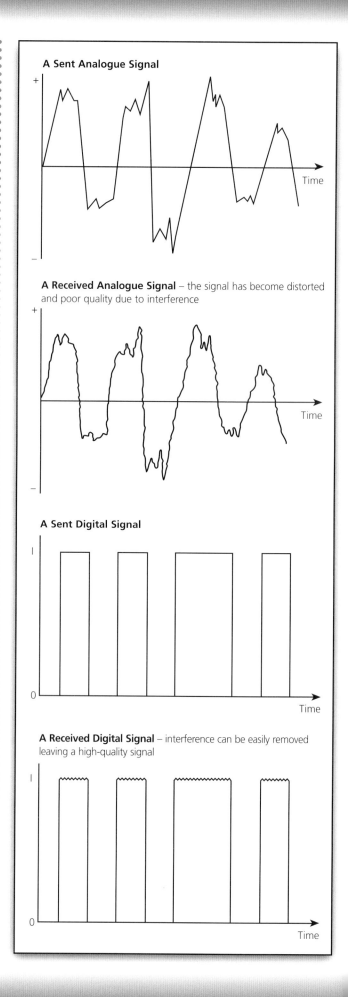

A Sent Analogue Signal

A Received Analogue Signal – the signal has become distorted and poor quality due to interference

A Sent Digital Signal

A Received Digital Signal – interference can be easily removed leaving a high-quality signal

Converting to Digital

Analogue signals use a continuous signal that can take any value; digital signals use a **binary** code where information is represented using two numeric values, i.e. 1 and 0. When converting from analogue to digital, the analogue signal is measured and converted into binary. The number of times the signal is measured per second is called the **sample rate**.

Low Sample Rate

When there is a low sample rate, few measurements are taken; only some information is taken from the original wave. Some information is, therefore, lost and sampling errors can be introduced, so the original wave will not be accurately reconstructed.

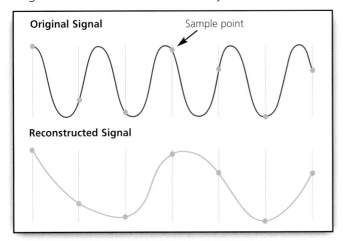

High Sample Rate

When there is a high sample rate, more information is taken from the original wave, which enables it to be reconstructed accurately. However, this type of sampling requires a large amount of data to be sent.

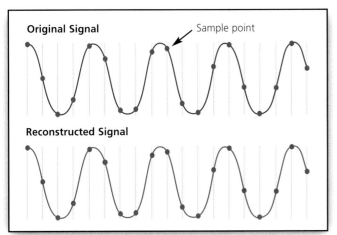

Each sample is converted into a **word** which is made up of a number of bits. A **bit** is one piece of information represented as either 1 or 0, and the **bit rate** is the number of bits that are sent per unit of time. One **byte** is equal to 8 bits of information.

When an analogue signal is sampled, the signal is rounded up or down to match the digital values available. More bits per word (a higher bit rate) will give finer detail and a closer representation of the original signal.

There is always a compromise involved when converting from analogue to digital, either in terms of the quality of the signal sent (a low or high sample rate) or the amount of data that is sent (a high or low bit rate).

Compression

A digital signal can be compressed in order to increase the speed at which it is sent. The compression process works by reducing the quantity of data sent. This can be done in a number of ways, for example, by removing redundant information, such as sounds that are too high pitched or too quiet for us to hear, or by using specific compression systems, e.g. MP3 or JPEG. Over-compressing a signal will result in a noticeable reduction in quality.

Signal Encryption

A signal in digital format can be easily manipulated using software. Many electronic systems are very similar and can therefore be mass-produced at a low cost. This helps to reduce the cost of the electronics used in digital communications.

Once produced, the system can be programmed for a particular job, e.g. encryption. Many systems use encryption programmes to increase security, for example, to protect information sent over a wireless computer network or to protect customers' details when they shop on the internet.

Communications

Sending Signals

Electrical signals can be transmitted from place to place in a variety of ways and forms, e.g. light, sound, etc. They can be carried…

- by radio waves with a range of frequencies
- in optical fibres by visible light and infrared
- in copper wires by an electric current.

The table at the foot of the page summarises different methods of transmitting signals.

The signal often needs to be converted from analogue to digital and back again. You need to be able to draw a block diagram to show how a message is sent from one place to another, identifying whether the signal is likely to be digital or analogue at each stage:

- If the signal is travelling in copper wire it is likely to be analogue.
- If the signal is travelling through an optical fibre it is likely to be digital. (See the examples opposite.)

When a computer receives an email it needs to be stored until it has been read. The information is stored on the computer's hard drive, but like any electronically stored information it could also be stored on a memory stick or burned to CD-ROM.

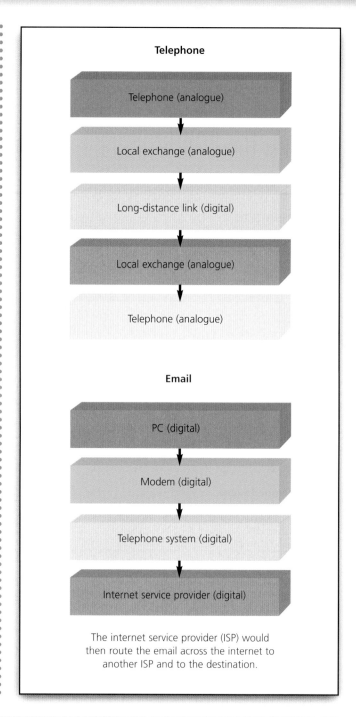

Telephone

Telephone (analogue)

↓

Local exchange (analogue)

↓

Long-distance link (digital)

↓

Local exchange (analogue)

↓

Telephone (analogue)

Email

PC (digital)

↓

Modem (digital)

↓

Telephone system (digital)

↓

Internet service provider (digital)

The internet service provider (ISP) would then route the email across the internet to another ISP and to the destination.

Link Type	Examples	Why Link Type is Used
Copper wire	• Local telephone system • Intercom system	Copper wire is relatively cheap and is suitable for the job. Receivers are fixed.
Optical fibre	• Long-distance telephone (transatlantic cable) • Computer network	Optical fibres can transmit data at a fast rate which increases the network speed.
Radio waves	• Mobile phone • Television	Radio waves allow for mobility so the receivers can be located anywhere within the transmitter's coverage.

Communication Signals

All communication systems transfer information from one point to another, normally between people. Many communications are based on shared signals, such as…

- visual symbols – hazard signs, flags
- sounds – air raid warnings, smoke alarms
- codes – Morse code, semaphore (a code based on using flags at different positions to represent letters).

Semaphore

When information is put into a type of code it is **encoded**. When the information is received at the other end and removed from the code it is **decoded**.

The **data transmission rate** is the amount of information that is transmitted in a given unit of time, from one space to another space. The percentage of pieces of information that contain mistakes is the **error rate**. The higher the error rate, the less reliable the connection or data transfer will be.

The **range** is the physical space over which the information can be sent, for example, the range for sending semaphore code depends on the visual distance that the code can be seen by another person.

Sending Images

Over the years, communication systems have become more sophisticated and complex and detailed information can now be sent very quickly. The transmission of pictures and videos is becoming increasingly common.

A single picture can be represented by rows of **pixels** (a single point in an image) making up a frame. For example, a standard computer resolution sets the screen as 1024 by 768. This makes a rectangle with 1024 pixels across the top and 768 pixels down the side, giving a total of 786 432 (1024 x 768) pixels in the frame.

A black and white picture requires 1 bit per pixel. To produce colour the word length per pixel needs to be increased. True colour uses words that are 32 bits long. This means that a single high-resolution true colour picture could be 25 165 824 bits (786 432 x 32), about 2.5Mbits (mega bits).

The video bit rate is also affected by the **refresh rate** (the number of pictures per second). A television has a refresh rate of 50Hz, i.e. 50 pictures per second. To receive true colour, a high-resolution television or computer could require a data transmission rate / bit rate of 125Mbits per second.

> **HT** Sending pictures and video information requires a very high bit and data transmission rate. So, in order for the information to be sent at a reasonable speed, the information can be compressed. Compressing the image will, however, lead to a reduction in the quality of the information. For example, video data sent over the internet is normally of a low quality.

Communications

Communication

The growth and improvements of communication technologies have greatly affected the way that we can communicate.

Hearing aids and digital technologies, for example, have increased the **quality** of communications.

The **quantity** of communication has been increased by the introduction of mobile phones (people can be contacted at any time) and broadband internet (more data can be sent and received at a faster rate).

Satellite communications and international television broadcasts have increased the distance of communications – telephone calls and television signals can now be sent to and from almost anywhere in the world.

Radio Waves

Radio waves are transmitted in the following way:

1. The original sound **signal**, containing the information, is converted into an electrical signal.
2. A weak signal can be amplified. An amplifier increases the amplitude of an alternating voltage (the signal) to make it stronger and clearer.
3. The signal is then added to a **carrier** wave. In order to do this, the wave must be **modulated** (varying either the amplitude or frequency). The carrier wave is modulated to give it a pattern that matches the signal.
4. The modulated wave is transmitted until it reaches the receiver, where the wave is demodulated and the original signal is recovered.

HT Radio waves can be modulated to either AM (amplitude modulation), or FM (frequency modulation). The signal causes either the amplitude of the carrier wave to change (AM) or the frequency of the carrier wave to change (FM).

The carrier wave then carries the signal when it is transmitted. The modulation process results in a number of frequencies being required to represent the signal. This range of frequencies is called the **bandwidth**.

Wave signal of FM (uniform amplitude, varying frequency)

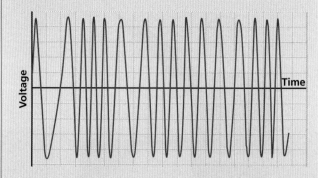

Wave signal of AM (uniform frequency, varying amplitude)

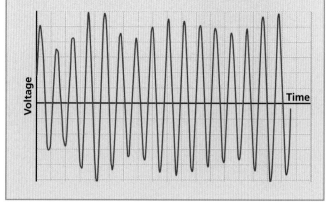

Transmitting a Signal

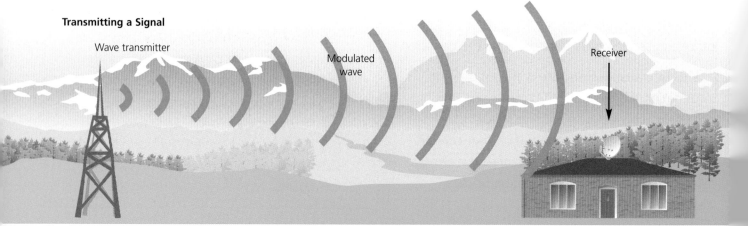

Wave transmitter

Modulated wave

Receiver

Wavelength

Radio waves can be reflected or absorbed by obstructions and the atmosphere; different wavelengths are reflected and absorbed by different amounts. Therefore, the frequency of a wave determines how it can be used in a communication system:

- Long wave radio (AM),150–300kHz.
- Medium wave radio (AM), 500kHz–1.5MHz.
- Very high frequency (VHF) Radio (FM), 90–110MHz.
- Terrestrial television, about 600MHz.
- Wi-fi / Bluetooth, about 2.4GHz.
- Mobile phones and satellite communications, about 10GHz.

Aerials

Different types of aerials are used for different wavelengths and devices.

Simple **dipole aerials** are used in car radios and walkie-talkies. They are made of a straight metal rod which can receive signals from all directions so they get a 360° reception.

Ferrite rods are used in radio receivers and mobile phones. They have a coil of wire wrapped around a ferrite rod in order to make the signal stronger.

Dish receivers are used in weather satellites, satellite phones and satellite televisions. They need to be pointing in the direction that the signal is coming from in order to pick it up.

Radio Receiver   **Satellite Television Dish**

Interference

Interference can occur when a radio receiver picks up more than one radio signal.

This interference could be due to different signals or radio waves that have come by different paths i.e. they are out of step.

If the waves are out of step, the peak of one can meet the trough of another and they can cancel each other out.

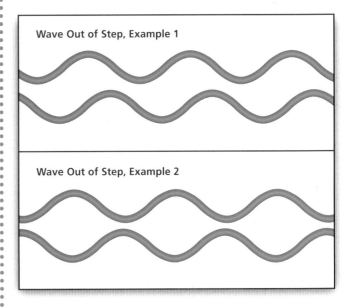

To help avoid interference, radio receivers are tuned to the specific broadcast frequency they are trying to receive as this tunes out the interfering waves.

Regulatory Organisations

Government organisations regulate the communications industries, for example, Ofcom regulates radio broadcasting in the UK.

Broadcasters need to obtain a licence to use part of the electromagnetic spectrum.

If they did not obtain a licence, different broadcasters could use the same frequencies as each other, leading to interference.

Governments create markets for competing telecommunications firms and agree standard protocols for messages so that they are compatible on different equipment and in different countries.

Communications

The Wave Equation

Wave speed, frequency and wavelength are related by the following equation:

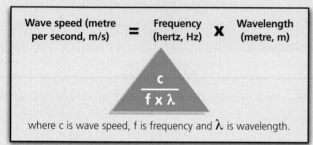

| Wave speed (metre per second, m/s) | = | Frequency (hertz, Hz) | X | Wavelength (metre, m) |

$$\frac{c}{f \times \lambda}$$

where c is wave speed, f is frequency and λ is wavelength.

Examples

1 A radio transmits signals with a wavelength of 200m at a speed of 300 000 000m/s. Calculate the frequency of the radio waves.

Rearrange the formula...

$$\text{Frequency} = \frac{\text{Wave speed}}{\text{Wavelength}}$$

$$= \frac{300\,000\,000 \text{m/s}}{200 \text{m}}$$

$$= \mathbf{1\,500\,000 Hz}$$

2 Radio 5 Live transmits on a frequency of 909 000Hz. If the speed of the radio waves is 300 000 000m/s, on what wavelength does it transmit?

Rearrange the formula...

$$\text{Wavelength} = \frac{\text{Wave speed}}{\text{Frequency}}$$

$$= \frac{300\,000\,000 \text{m/s}}{909\,000 \text{Hz}}$$

$$= \mathbf{330m}$$

Diffraction

Radio waves can be diffracted when passing obstacles, e.g. hills and buildings.

When radio waves move through an aperture (gap), e.g. through or around buildings and hills, they can be diffracted, i.e. they spread out from the edges.

Diffraction is most obvious when the aperture is similar in size to, or smaller than, the wavelength.

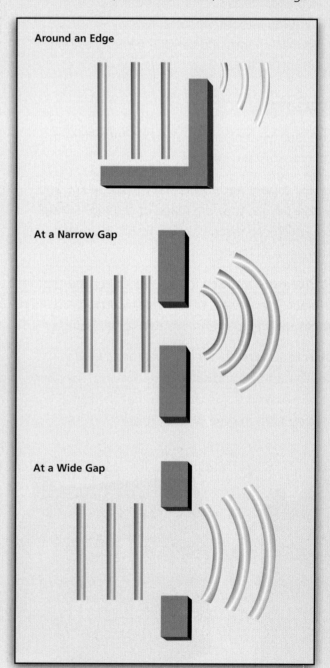

Around an Edge

At a Narrow Gap

At a Wide Gap

Communications

Television Broadcasts

Creating a television broadcast, especially a live, outside broadcast, is a very complex process. It requires staff with a wide range of technical expertise, who can manage and use equipment effectively.

The diagram below illustrates the main stages and staff involved in recording a broadcast:

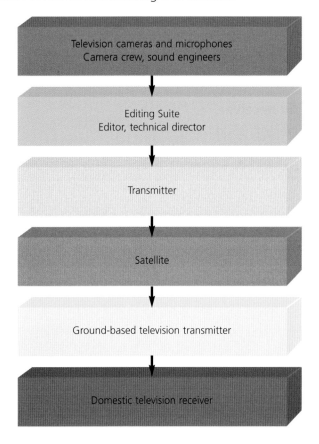

Television cameras and microphones
Camera crew, sound engineers

↓

Editing Suite
Editor, technical director

↓

Transmitter

↓

Satellite

↓

Ground-based television transmitter

↓

Domestic television receiver

Wireless Communications

Wireless communications include mobile phones, walkie-talkies, bluetooth, radio and television. These communication methods use electromagnetic waves, usually microwaves and radio waves.

A radio communications system can be represented by the following blocks:

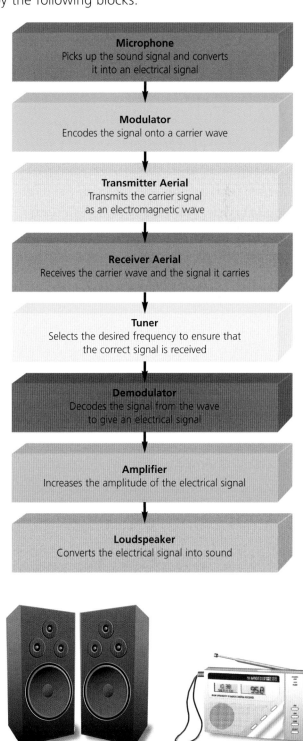

Microphone
Picks up the sound signal and converts it into an electrical signal

↓

Modulator
Encodes the signal onto a carrier wave

↓

Transmitter Aerial
Transmits the carrier signal as an electromagnetic wave

↓

Receiver Aerial
Receives the carrier wave and the signal it carries

↓

Tuner
Selects the desired frequency to ensure that the correct signal is received

↓

Demodulator
Decodes the signal from the wave to give an electrical signal

↓

Amplifier
Increases the amplitude of the electrical signal

↓

Loudspeaker
Converts the electrical signal into sound

Communications

Design and Manufacture

There are several key factors of a product specification to consider when designing a communications system:

- range of functions
- range of controls
- sound or image quality
- power output
- type of power source
- size
- weight
- network coverage
- components that can be recycled
- cost.

Comparing the product specification with the customer's requirements and selecting the most appropriate system also requires the following factors to be considered:

- acceptable cost
- likely customers
- available technology
- current fashion
- expected lifetime
- profit margin.

Example

A communications system is needed for staff working at a major sporting event.

They will need to be able to communicate quickly and easily from various places. Several systems are being considered. Which is the most suitable: wireless intercom, mobile phone or radio receiver?

Wireless Intercom

- Weight: 1.1kg
- Size: 95mm x 210mm x 80mm
- Talk time: unlimited
- Power supply: 230V ac
- Range: up to 250m
- Functions: paging system
- Cost: buying and installing the system.

Mobile Phone

- Weight: 116.6g
- Size: 117mm x 49mm x 24mm
- Talk time: approximately 350 minutes
- Power supply: rechargeable battery
- Range: unlimited
- Functions: personalised messaging; bluetooth wireless technology; digital camera with a 4x zoom; a 500-entry phone book; picture caller ID; WAP 2.0 for internet access; 22KHz speaker.
- Cost: purchase price of the phone, monthly tariffs (fees) and call charges.

Radio Receiver

- Weight: 350g
- Size: 160mm x 140mm x 48mm
- Talk time: approximately 300 minutes
- Range: up to 250m
- Power supply: rechargeable battery
- Functions: interference rejection; integrated transmitter and receiver circuitry; can use any channel in 100kHz steps.
- Cost: purchase price of the receivers.

The wireless intercom requires a mains supply so could not be used by staff working away from the base.

The mobile phone is a good option, but it would be quite costly as there is a monthly fee, not all the features would be needed, and there is always a time delay as a call is connected.

Therefore, in this example, the radio receiver would be the best choice as it is portable, not too heavy and has a suitable range.

Detecting Faults

A voltmeter is a simple piece of equipment that can be used to detect faults in a communication system.

The voltmeter is connected in parallel with the component or group of components, and the voltage across the components is measured. For example, the diagram below shows a processor block under test.

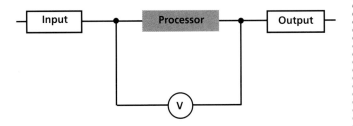

When testing, if the reading of the voltmeter is not what it should be, then the engineer knows there is a fault and can choose to replace the faulty block.

HT Signals between blocks can be measured and compared with the expected signal. This can be done by putting a known test signal into a system.

By measuring the signal between each block and comparing it with the expected signal the faulty block in a system can be determined.

Oscilloscopes

An oscilloscope can be used to measure the amplitude and frequency of a time-varying signal.

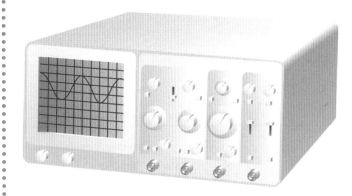

The graph below shows an oscilloscope trace:

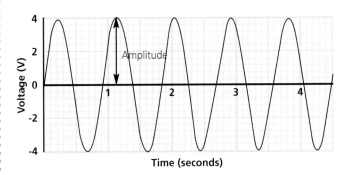

The amplitude of the wave is measured from the middle point to the peak. In the example above, the amplitude is 4 volts.

The graph shows that one wave is completed every 9ms (0.9s). To find the frequency (the number of complete waves in a second) divide 1 by the time it takes to complete a wave.

Frequency $= \dfrac{1}{0.9}$

$\quad\quad\quad = \textbf{1.1Hz}$.

Communications

Health and Safety

There are potential hazards in any situation where electricity is used. Regulatory bodies such as the British Standards Institution (BSI) and the European Committee for Standardization (CE) use safety symbols which are designed to warn workers and the public in order to safeguard their health.

Emergency Stop

First Aid Point

Electrical Shock Hazard – 230V

BSI Kitemark

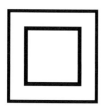

Double Insulated

Earth Connection

Danger

Laser

Safety Features

Electrical and electronic equipment is fitted with a range of features to help make it safe to use, for example…

- **double insulation** – individual cables in a wire are insulated and then wrapped in a second layer of insulation
- **over-current device** – trips the switch / fuse and breaks the circuit if too much current flows.

> **Earth leakage devices** are designed to break a circuit and cut out the supply if a potentially dangerous fault causes a current to flow down the earth wire.

You need to be able to identify the potential electrical hazards in a given situation and suggest ways of controlling the risk.

For example, when using a set of hedge trimmers, there is the danger of cutting through the cable. This risk can be reduced by…

- taking extra care when using the trimmers
- using a socket fitted with a circuit breaker.

Materials and Performance

Module Ap6

Materials are selected for use depending on their properties and the way they behave. This module looks at…

- the properties and uses of materials
- elastic and plastic strength
- the behaviour of materials
- forces
- sounds and sound levels
- mirrors and lenses.

Choosing Materials

A good knowledge of materials and their properties is essential for many people working in industry, research or standards. For example, a mechanical engineer or an architect must be able to select the correct material for the job, taking into account details such as durability, cost, environmental impact, appearance and other specific properties, e.g. strength.

Classes of Materials

The main classes of materials are listed below:

- **Metals and alloys** – good conductors of heat and electricity, shiny, stiff, ductile and malleable. Examples: steel, copper and aluminium.
- **Polymers** – insulators of heat and electricity, often flexible and / or plastic. Examples: polystyrene, polyethylene and polythene.
- **Ceramics** – insulators of heat and electricity, stiff, brittle. Example: glass.
- **Woods and wood products** – examples: MDF, pine and chipboard.
- **Composites** – examples: carbon fibre, fibreglass and Kevlar.

Maintaining and Enforcing Standards

It is important to monitor standardisation in order to ensure safety, quality and consistency of products. Organisations that set product standards include the **British Standards Institution (BSI)** and the **European Committee for Standardization (CE)**. Only products that meet their standards are allowed to display their symbols. The **International Organization for Standardization (ISO)** develops voluntary International Standards.

| BSI | CE | ISO |

Artefacts (products) are designed with **safety margins** and it is the job of certain practitioners to enforce these safety standards and take action when they are not met.

For example, a trading standards officer may have to ensure that children's clothing meets the British Standards requirements for being fire-retardant, and that toys for very young children do not have small parts that could be a choking hazard.

A buildings control surveyor must inspect new buildings to ensure they are safe and of sound construction, e.g. they can withstand strong winds without suffering structural damage, and that the roof is strong enough to withstand a build-up of snow, etc.

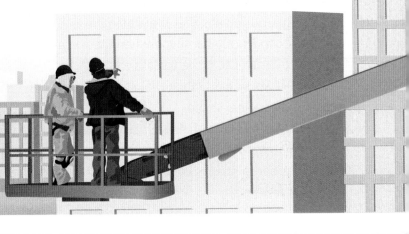

Materials and Performance

Mechanical Behaviour of Materials

The mechanical properties of a material are described using the following terms:

- **Stiffness / flexibility** – describes how resistant a material is to bending; a material with a high stiffness will not bend easily (flexibility is the opposite of stiffness). For example, a wall needs to be stiff, whilst bag straps need to be flexible.
- **Toughness / brittleness** – describes how resistant a material is to snapping. Tough materials will not snap or shatter easily (brittleness is the opposite of toughness). For example, ordinary glass is brittle, toughened glass is not.
- **Density** – describes how heavy a certain volume of material is. If two objects are of the same size but have different densities, the one made of a denser material will have a greater mass.
- **Tensile (breaking) strength** – describes how much force is needed to break a material when loaded under tension. For example, climbing ropes need high tensile strength in order to support the climber.
- **Compressive strength** – describes the maximum force a material can withstand before fracturing when loaded under compression. For example, building bricks need a high compressive strength because they have to bear the load of the building above them.
- **Elastic or plastic** – when a force is applied to a material it can show elastic or plastic behaviour. Elastic behaviour means that the material will spring back to its original shape when the force is removed. However, if the force is too high the material will show plastic behaviour and will not return to its original shape.
- **Hardness** – a hard material is difficult to scratch, a softer material will scratch more easily. For example, a bar of soap is very soft, whilst a piece of steel is very hard.

Examples of Hardness

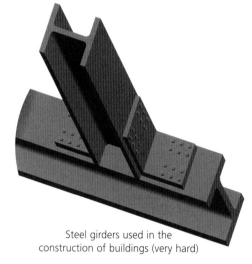

Steel girders used in the construction of buildings (very hard)

Soap (soft)

HT The mechanical properties of a material can be affected by temperature, for example, heating a metal will reduce its stiffness and low temperatures can increase brittleness.

The mechanical properties of a material are very important when designing a product.

Some artefacts use materials which are selected for their mechanical behaviour, such as...
- flexible clothing that changes shape as the wearer moves
- body-shaping mattresses which adjust to the shape of the user in order to provide increased comfort.

Some artefacts have materials which are selected for their complementary mechanical behaviour, such as...
- cycle helmets which have a force-spreading outer shell and an energy-absorbing inner lining
- cushions which have a flexible outer layer and a soft filling.

Materials and Performance

Improving Mechanical Properties

The mechanical properties of a material can be improved by combining it with other materials in different ways, for example, to make alloys or composites.

An **alloy** is made by mixing a molten metal with other elements (often other metals). The elements in the mixture dissolve, creating a solution, and when this cools it forms a solid solution.

Different mixes are used to give alloys different properties. Alloys can have benefits over pure metals, for example, in terms of hardness, tensile strength, melting point or resistance to corrosion.

A **composite material** is a mix where one material is embedded into another, e.g. fibres in a resin (the resin holds the fibres in a pattern called a matrix). The two most common composites are…
* fibre-glass composites (used in boat hulls)
* carbon-fibre composites (used in Formula One cars).

HT Composite materials are designed to combine the useful properties of different materials while avoiding their drawbacks.

For example:
* Fibre-glass is a composite of glass and resin. The glass provides stiffness, whilst the resin gives it toughness and makes it lightweight.
* Kevlar® is a polymer used in many composite materials. It can be used to add toughness and stiffness to many artefacts.

Improving Structures

A structure can be designed to have better mechanical properties than its component parts, for example, by increasing its strength and stiffness and reducing its density.

A product can be made more rigid by…
* increasing the thickness of the material
* using stronger or stiffer materials
* changing the structure, e.g. using a triangular structure rather than a flat one because a triangular structure uses compressive and tensile strength as well as stiffness.

Evaluating Materials

Before a material is used to make a product, several factors need to be evaluated:
* Properties – does it have the properties required?
* Cost – is it affordable?
* Durability – how long will it last?
* Environmental impact – what impact could the material have during manufacture, use or disposal?
* Aesthetic appeal – does it look good?

Example
What material should be used to make a tennis racket – steel, wood or carbon fibre?

Steel would be very strong and long-lasting but would be too heavy for practical use.

Wood would be an acceptable choice in terms of cost, although it might not be as strong or durable as the other options.

Carbon fibre is lighter and stronger than steel but is more expensive to produce.

The user of the racket therefore also needs to be considered, e.g. if the racket is going to be used by a professional tennis player then performance would be a more important consideration than cost, and so carbon fibre would be a good choice.

HT It is often the combination of properties that makes a material suitable for a particular job. For example, the bases of frying pans are made of copper, which is a good conductor of heat and has a high melting point. Carbon fibres are used for making bicycle frames because they are very light and very strong.

Materials and Performance

Describing Materials

Samples of materials can be described by their...
- electrical conductance
- thermal conductance
- thermal expansion.

Electrical Conductance

The electrical conductance of a material is a measure of how easy it is for electricity to flow through it (it is the opposite of resistance). For example, copper has a high conductance while plastic has a low conductance.

The conductance of an artefact depends not only on the conductivity of the material it is made from, but also its shape (length and thickness), e.g. a thick wire has more conductivity than a thin wire.

When creating electrical fittings, the mechanical and electrical properties of a material need to be considered. For example, in a television...
- the wire in a cable needs to be flexible and have a high conductance
- the outer sleeve of the cable needs to be flexible and have a very low conductance
- the pins of the plug need to have a high conductance and be very rigid.

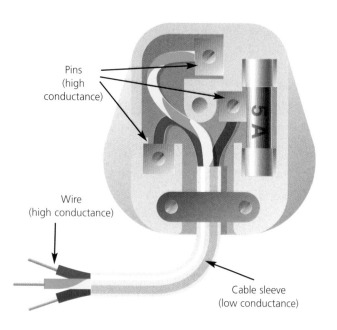

Pins
(high
conductance)

Wire
(high conductance)

Cable sleeve
(low conductance)

HT The electrical conductance of a material can be measured by connecting an ammeter in series and a voltmeter in parallel in a circuit (see diagram below).

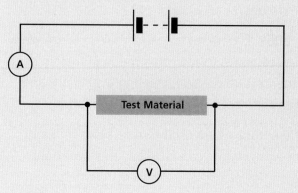

Readings can then be taken from the meters and used to find the conductance using this formula:

$$\text{Conductance (Siemens)} = \frac{\text{Current (amps)}}{\text{Voltage (volts)}}$$

Example
The electrical conductance of a piece of copper is being tested. If the current is 18A and voltage 3V, calculate the conductance.

$$\text{Conductance} = \frac{18V}{3A} = \textbf{6 Siemens}$$

If measurements are made at a variety of voltages, a graph of current against voltage can be plotted. Calculating the gradient of the graph will then give the conductance. For example, the graph below shows the electrical conduction of two materials.

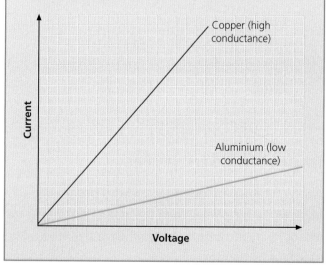

Copper (high conductance)

Aluminium (low conductance)

Current

Voltage

Materials and Performance

Thermal Conductance

The **thermal conductance** of a material describes how easy it is for heat to flow through it. A material with a low thermal conductance will feel warmer than one with a high thermal conductance, when both are at the same temperature.

For example, if a person touches a piece of wood and a piece of copper that are the same temperature, the wood feels warmer because it does not allow heat through it easily, so the hand loses heat slowly. The copper allows heat through it easily so the hand loses heat quickly and the copper feels colder.

Thermal conductance is an important consideration when selecting which materials are best suited to a specific purpose. Building materials need to be strong, but it is often desirable for them to have low thermal conductance. In this way, less heat will be lost from the building (through windows, doors, the roof, etc.) and heating costs would be reduced.

Thermal Expansion

When an object increases in temperature it expands; this is **thermal expansion**. To measure thermal expansion, fix one end of the sample in a clamp and rest the other end on a solid block. A pin attached to a rotating pointer sits between the sample and the solid block. As the sample is heated, it expands causing the pin to rotate and the pointer to move. The sample which causes the largest movement on the scale in a certain time has the greatest thermal expansion.

Copper – high thermal conductance

Wood – low thermal conductance

Thermal Expansion Experiment

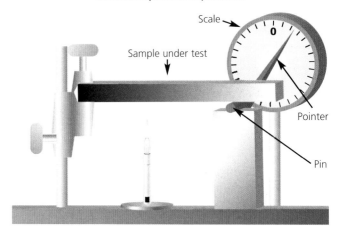

Scale

Sample under test

Pointer

Pin

HT Sometimes materials are selected because they have thermal properties that match other parts of the product. For example:
- A camera body needs to have the same thermal properties for all of its parts so that expansion does not cause gaps in the case which would expose the film.
- The piston and cylinders in an engine need to expand at the same rate.

Sometimes, materials are selected because their properties complement one another, for example:
- A bi-metallic strip has two different metals which expand at different rates causing the strip to bend as the temperature changes. This is used in some kettles to turn them off when the water has reached boiling point.
- A frying pan has a conducting base but an insulating handle.

Materials and Performance

Measuring Stiffness

Stiffness between different materials can be compared in a school laboratory using the following experiment:

The material to be tested is supported at each end by two clamps. Weights are then gradually loaded onto the middle of the material. The weights will eventually cause the material to bend, and the weight needed to produce a fixed amount of bending is recorded.

The test is repeated with different materials (all materials must have the same dimensions). The material that needs the largest weight in order to make it bend a fixed amount is the stiffest.

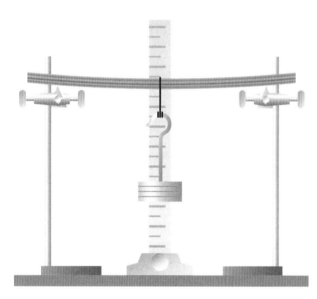

A similar method can be used where the material is clamped at one end, and weights are applied to the opposite end. The weight that is needed in order to make the end of the material bend is recorded.

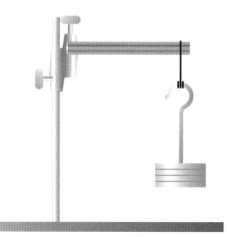

Measuring Strength

Measuring compressive or tensile strength involves increasing the load on a material until it fractures (compressive strength) or snaps (tensile strength). The diagrams below show the equipment that would be used in school laboratories for each test.

Compressive

The solid block of material to be tested is placed on a metal block. Weights are then added to the top of the material. As the force increases, the material will eventually fracture. The weight needed to fracture the material is recorded.

The test is repeated with different materials (all materials must have the same dimensions). The material that needs the largest weight in order to make it fracture has the biggest compressive strength.

Tensile

The piece of wire to be tested is stretched between a clamp and a pulley wheel. Weights are added onto the end of the wire which increases the stretching force. Eventually, the breaking strain of the wire will be reached and the wire will snap. The weight needed to snap the wire is recorded.

The test is repeated with different types of wire (all pieces of wire need to be the same length and width). The wire that needs the largest weight in order to make it snap has the biggest tensile strength.

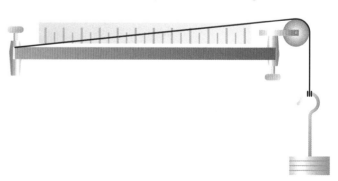

Force–Extension Graphs

A force–extension graph shows how a material stretches when it is under tensile stress. The behaviour of a material can be predicted by looking carefully at these graphs.

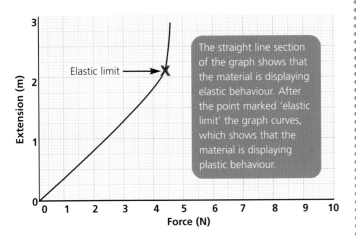

The straight line section of the graph shows that the material is displaying elastic behaviour. After the point marked 'elastic limit' the graph curves, which shows that the material is displaying plastic behaviour.

HT A force–extension graph can be used to calculate the energy stored (J) in a stretched sample and predict the extension of a given force.

The energy stored in a stretched sample can be shown by calculating the area under the graph. For example, in the graph above, if the force is 3N, the energy stored would be: $\frac{3 \times 1.25}{2} = 1.88J$

As long as the elastic limit has not been reached the extension for any given force can be predicted, using the formula below.

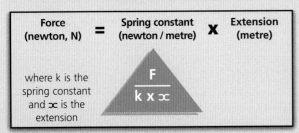

| Force (newton, N) | = | Spring constant (newton / metre) | X | Extension (metre) |

where k is the spring constant and x is the extension

$$\frac{F}{k \times x}$$

N.B. The gradient of the graph is the spring constant (k).

Example
A spring has a spring constant of 50N/m. If there is a force of 4N, calculate the extension.

$$\text{Extension} = \frac{\text{Force}}{\text{Spring constant}}$$

$$= \frac{4N}{50N/m} = \textbf{0.08m (8cm)}$$

When analysing data you need to be able to spot outliers, make a conclusion and comment on the quality of the data.

Example
The following data was collected in an experiment as a force was applied to a spring. What can you conclude?

Force (N)	Extension (cm)			
	1st Attempt	2nd Attempt	3rd Attempt	Average
1	2.1	1.9	2.9	2.0
2	3.8	4.0	4.2	4.0
3	6.4	6.7	6.7	6.6
4	8.0	8.1	7.9	8.0
5	10.0	9.6	9.8	9.8

It can be seen that the 3rd attempt at 1N has a value that is significantly different from the other two attempts. This anomalous result is called an **outlier** and is not included in the calculation to find the average. The results can be plotted on a graph.

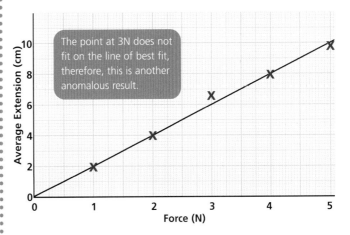

The point at 3N does not fit on the line of best fit, therefore, this is another anomalous result.

From these results we can conclude that the spring behaves elastically and that every 1N increase in force causes a 2cm increase in length. There were a few anomalies, so the data may not be completely accurate. We do not know what would happen after a force of 5N, and we do not know when the elastic limit will be reached. Further tests would need to be carried out to confirm this.

Materials and Performance

Responding to Forces

The **velocity** of an object is the rate of change of distance in a particular direction. The **momentum** of an object is proportional to both mass and velocity. When forces act on a body they will often cause its velocity to change.

If a **resultant force** acts on an object, it causes a change in momentum in the direction of the force.

If the resultant force acting on an object is zero its momentum will not change. If the object…
- is stationary, it will remain stationary
- is already moving, it will continue moving in a straight line at a constant speed.

If the resultant force acting on an object is not zero, it causes a change in momentum in the direction of the force. This could…
- give a stationary object momentum (i.e. make it start to move)
- increase or decrease the speed, or change the direction, of a moving object, i.e. change its velocity.

The size of change in momentum depends on…
- the size of the resultant force
- the length of time the force is acting on the object.

Collisions

If a car is involved in a collision it comes to a sudden stop, i.e. it undergoes a rapid change in momentum. This sudden change in momentum will affect not only the vehicle but also the occupants, who will experience a large force which can lead to serious injuries.

If the change in momentum is spread out over a longer period of time, the force experienced by the occupants of the car will be much smaller.

Road safety devices, e.g. seat-belts, crumple zones, and cycle and motorcycle helmets are designed to increase the time over which momentum changes.

Helmet inners are made from expanded polystyrene because it plastically deforms to absorb the energy of the impact. Seat-belts are made from tightly woven thick polyester which makes them flexible and comfortable to use, but they have a high tensile strength so they do not snap.

HT A graph of force against time shows how the force on an object varies with time. The graph below shows the collision of two cars. Car A has a standard crumple zone, and car B has an advanced crumple zone.

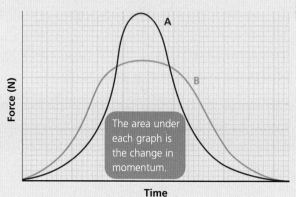

The area under each graph is the change in momentum.

When the collision takes a longer time to occur, as in car B, the force must be lower.

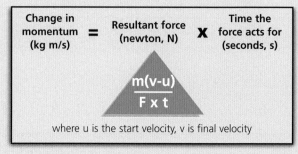

| Change in momentum (kg m/s) | = | Resultant force (newton, N) | X | Time the force acts for (seconds, s) |

$$\frac{m(v-u)}{F \times t}$$

where u is the start velocity, v is final velocity

Example

A 1000kg car travelling at 30m/s is involved in an accident and comes to a halt in 0.1 seconds. What is the force acting on the occupants during the accident?

$$\text{Resultant force} = \frac{\text{Change in momentum}}{\text{Time the force acts for}}$$

$$= \frac{30\,000\text{kg m/s}}{0.1\text{s}} = \textbf{300\,000N}$$

Materials and Performance

Acoustics

When an object vibrates it produces sound, e.g. a tuning fork. Different tuning forks will produce different notes because they vibrate at different frequencies; a rapid vibration has a high frequency and produces a high-pitched sound.

If a tuning fork is struck hard it produces a louder sound because the amplitude of the vibration is bigger. A large vibration will produce a louder sound than a small vibration.

How loud a sound is depends on the sensitivity of the ear and the frequency of the sound. The human ear is most sensitive to sounds around 2000Hz (2kHz). Some sounds are so high or so low pitched that the human ear cannot detect them at all.

The decibel scale is used to describe sound intensity; it is not a linear scale. Increasing a sound by 10 decibels (dB) doubles its loudness. Therefore, a sound measured at 40dB is twice as loud as 30dB, four times as loud as 20dB, and eight times as loud as 10dB.

Reducing Sound Levels

Prolonged exposure to loud sounds can cause permanent hearing loss or tinnitus (ringing in the ears). There are, therefore, various methods, and materials, that can be used to reduce or absorb sound.

The sound entering a building can be either absorbed or reflected. Hard materials, such as the glass in double glazing, are good at reflecting sound. This makes double glazing popular in urban environments, and helps to reduce sleep loss and associated problems. Porous materials, such as carpet underlay and acoustic tiles, reduce sound intensity by absorbing it.

Buildings can be damaged by vibrations caused by machinery. This damage can be prevented by mounting the machinery on springs or shock absorbers. In some laboratories even the slightest vibration can cause a problem with an experiment or production process. To reduce these vibrations the entire floor can be supported on fluid-filled dampers.

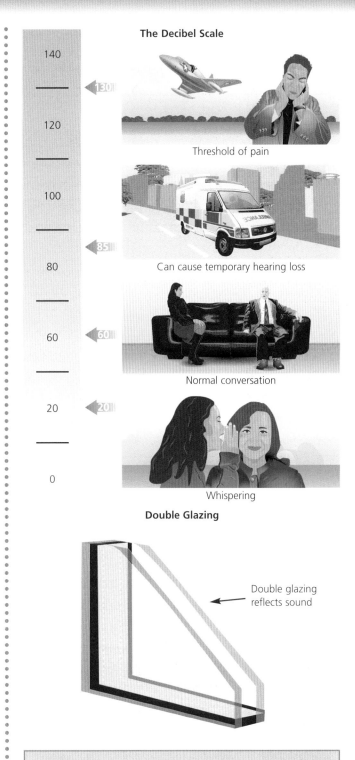

The Decibel Scale

140

130

120

100

85

80

Can cause temporary hearing loss

Threshold of pain

60

60

Normal conversation

20

20

0

Whispering

Double Glazing

Double glazing reflects sound

HT Due to their size, buildings have a low resonant frequency which makes them particularly susceptible to low frequency vibrations. The low frequency can set up resonance in the building where the vibrations get larger and larger until the structure fails. When trying to protect buildings it is these frequency sounds in particular that need to be reduced.

Materials and Performance

Optical Behaviour

How light interacts with a material depends on the material's optical properties.

To accurately describe the optical behaviour of a material you need to use and understand the following terms:

- **Transparent** – a material which lets light pass through virtually unchanged; the rays of light remain coherent as they pass through the material.
- **Reflective** – a surface that reflects (bounces) light off it. The more reflective the surface, the greater the amount of light that bounces off it.
- **Translucent** – allows light to pass through but jumbles it up; the light rays become incoherent, you cannot see details through a translucent material.
- **Opaque** – does not let light through.
- **Refraction** – light passing from one material to another changes direction as it crosses the boundary between the materials.

*N.B. Coloured glass is **not** translucent. It is transparent to the colour it lets through and opaque to other colours.*

Using Glass

Glass can be used in many artefacts. Its use depends on its optical properties and other properties (mechanical, thermal, etc). These additional requirements have led to the development of a range of specialised glass. For example:

- Toughened glass is used for car windows as it will not shatter into sharp fragments in the event of an accident.
- Photochromic glass is used in sunglasses as it changes in darkness in response to light intensity.

> **HT** The glass used for **optical fibres** must be extremely pure as any impurities could cause the light travelling down the fibre to be absorbed.
>
> As some fibres are hundreds or even thousands of kilometres long, even a low level of impurity could absorb a large proportion of the signal.
>
> **Contact lenses** need to be made of transparent materials, but they also need to be...
> - gas permeable
> - easily sterilised
> - un-reactive
> - tough
> - able to stick to tears.

Using Mirrors

Mirrors can be used in a variety of ways. Plane mirrors are used for reflections, whilst curved mirrors can be used in optical instruments such as telescopes or to give unusual reflections (like in a hall of mirrors at a fairground).

Lenses

Most lenses are made out of glass but some polymers (plastics) can also be used. Some specialised glass is used, for example, in thin and light lenses.

Light can be partially reflected at the surface of glass (for example, you can see your reflection when looking out of a window at night). To prevent this reflection occurring in cameras, a special coating is added to the lens which allows more light to be transmitted through it.

The behaviour of light rays depends on the type of lens used.

A **diverging lens** is concave; it causes rays of light passing through it to spread out.

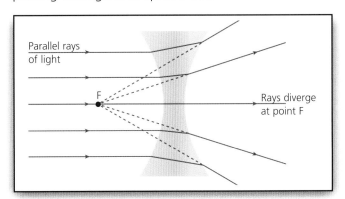

A **converging lens** is convex; rays of light passing through it are bent inwards. Rays of light coming from a distant object are effectively parallel, and a convex lens will bring these rays inwards to focus an image of the object in the focal plane, as shown in the diagram below.

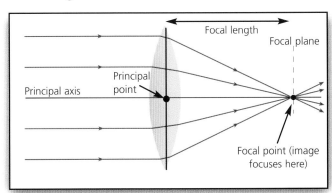

The power of the lens is measured in Dioptres. A more powerful lens will have a shorter focal length and will focus the image closer to the lens.

Describing Images

Images can be described by the following terms which compare them to the object:

- Real – a real image can be formed when rays of light actually meet; can be focused on a screen.
- Virtual – a virtual image is where rays of light appear to come from the image; cannot be focused on a screen.
- Inverted – upside down.
- Upright – the right way up.

The table below shows the general characteristics of images produced by some common optical devices when used in the normal way.

Device	Image Characteristics
Eye	• Real • Inverted • Smaller than object
Camera	• Real • Inverted • Smaller than object
Projector	• Real • Upright • Larger than object
Magnifying Glass	• Virtual • Inverted • Larger than object

Placing an object at different distances from the instrument can change how the image behaves. For example, using a magnifying glass with a distant object will produce an image that is real, inverted and smaller. You need to compare the image with the object to be able to say what the instrument has done.

Materials and Performance

A Camera

A simple camera works in a very similar way to the human eye.

1. Lens – focuses the light from the object.
2. Shutter – prevents light from entering the camera; opens to expose the film when a picture is taken.
3. Aperture – controls the amount of light entering when the shutter is opened.
4. Focal plane – the film is placed here and the image is focused on it.
5. Viewfinder – shows what the photo will look like.

A lens works because refraction occurs at the surface when light rays enter and leave the lens. One way to change the degree of refraction is to change the curvature of the lens; a greater curve will produce a shorter focal length. The **refractive index** of a material is a measure of how much it bends light rays. Using materials with a different refractive index is another way to change the focal length of the lens.

When a distant object is moved closer to a camera or the eye, the image becomes larger but moves beyond the focal length. This movement means that the image is no longer focused on the focal plane (i.e. the camera film or the retina) and would be blurry.

The human eye maintains focus by making the lens fatter in order to decrease its focal length; this makes it more curved. It is not practical to keep changing the lens in the camera so the camera maintains focus by moving the lens towards the object (away from the film).

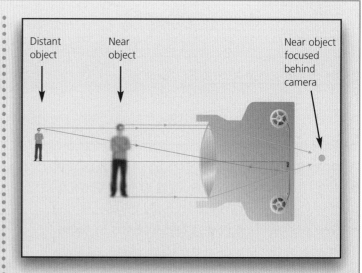

Distant object | Near object | Near object focused behind camera

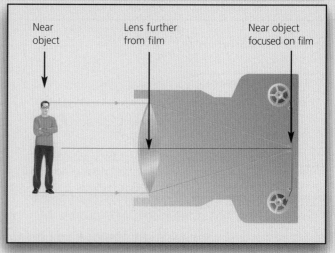

Near object | Lens further from film | Near object focused on film

Analogue – a signal which can take any value

Binary – a code which represents information using 2 numeric values (1s or 0s)

Bit – a single piece of information represented as either 1 or 0

Bit rate – the number of bits sent per unit of time

Byte – 8 bits

Carrier wave – a wave that carries the signal

Composite material – one material embedded into another

Compression – a force which presses down on, and around, a material

Compressive strength – the maximum force a material can withstand before it breaks when loaded under compression

Converging lens – a lens that causes light rays passing through it to meet at a point

Data transmission rate – the amount of information transmitted in a given unit of time

Decoding – taking information out of a coded signal

Diffraction – a change in the direction of a wave at the edge of an obstacle in its path

Digital – a signal which has two states: on and off

Diverging lens – a lens that causes light rays passing though it to be spread out

Elastic behaviour – a material that springs back into shape after a force has been applied

Electrical conductance – a measure of how easily electricity flows through a material

Encoding – putting information into a coded signal

Error rate – the percentage of transmitted information that contains mistakes

Focal length – a measure of how strongly an optical system focuses or diverges

Focal plane – a point where images are focused

Frequency – the number of waves produced within a given time period

Image – a representation of an object

Input – a device where data is collected

Interference – the noise created when a receiver picks up more than one signal

Inverted – an image which is upside down

Modulation – changing the amplitude or frequency of a carrier wave by adding a signal

Oscilloscope – a piece of equipment used to measure the amplitude and frequency of a signal

Output – a device which converts a processed signal into an understandable format

Parallel circuit – an electronic circuit which has more than one path for the current to take

Pitch – how high or low a sound is (changes with frequency)

Plastic behaviour – property of a material that does not return to its original shape after a force has been applied

Processor – manipulates and changes information

Range – the physical space over which information can be sent

Real image – image that can be focused on a screen

Reflection – a wave thrown back from a surface

Refraction – the change in direction of a wave as it passes from one medium to another

Resultant force – the total force acting on an object

Sample rate – the number of times a signal is measured per second

Series circuit – an electronic circuit where there is only one path for the current to take

Signal – an electronic signal containing information

Tensile strength – describes how much stretching force is needed to break a material loaded under tension

Tension – a force related to the stretching of an object

Thermal conductance – a measure of how easily heat flows through a material

Thermal expansion – the rate a material expands as a result of an increase in temperature

Upright – an image which is the right way up

Velocity – the speed and direction of an object

Virtual image – image that cannot be focused on a screen

Voltmeter – a piece of equipment used to detect faults in a communication system

Word – a number of bits that are used to carry information about something, e.g. pixels

Assessment Objectives

Assessment Objectives

Your final mark and grade for OCR GCSE Additional Applied Science will be based on three sets of criteria called **Assessment Objectives (AO)**.

These assessment objectives are set out on the opposite page so that you can see what the examiner and your teacher(s) will be looking for when they mark your test papers and portfolio. Definitions for some of the more difficult words and phrases are given below:

Scientific evidence – results of an experiment, or facts that can be used to prove or disprove a theory
Scientific explanations – scientific concepts that provide a framework for making sense of the world
Scientific theories – suggested explanations for something, often based on a combination of observations, existing scientific knowledge and a bit of creative thinking
Validated – checked and proven to be relevant and accurate
Ethical issues – issues concerned with what is morally right and wrong
Evaluate – to determine the worth or effectiveness of a conclusion by judging the quality of the evidence

First-hand data – data that you collect yourself, e.g. through observations, measurements or experiments
Secondary data – data that has been collected and presented by someone other than yourself
Analyse – to look at in detail
Interpret – to explain the meaning of
Qualitative – a test or measurement which uses observation and involves sensory comparison
Quantitative – a test or measurement which produces a numerical value and does not depend on the sensory skill of the observor
Validity – concerned with the reliability and relevance of something, e.g. scientific evidence
Reliability – concerned with how trustworthy or dependable something is. Scientific data is normally regarded as reliable if it can be reproduced by following the same procedure
Justifying – showing or proving that something is accurate

The Modular Tests

In your three modular tests, you will be marked on Assessment Objectives 1 and 2 only (see opposite). It is important that you learn and understand all the scientific facts, ideas and terms covered in this revision guide (AO1), but it is just as important that you can apply this knowledge and use it to form arguments, draw conclusions, solve problems and understand information relating to practices and procedures that you may not have heard of before (AO2).

Applying knowledge is a skill. It cannot be memorised or revised. However, it can be developed and improved through practice.

On the following pages are some sample questions to help you practise and develop this skill. Write your answers on a separate sheet of paper and then use the **answers** and **comments** that follow to check your work.

The workbook that supports this revision guide contains more tasks and questions that will help you to practise applying your scientific knowledge.

Assessment Objectives

Assessment Objective 1 (AO1): Knowledge and understanding of how science works

- You must demonstrate that you have learned and now understand the scientific facts, concepts, techniques and vocabulary in the specification.
- You must show that you understand how scientific evidence is collected and the relationship between **scientific evidence** and **scientific explanations and theories**.
- You must show that you understand the process by which scientific knowledge and ideas change over time, and how these changes are **validated**.

Assessment Objective 2 (AO2): Application of skills, knowledge and understanding

- You must be able to use your scientific knowledge to develop arguments and draw conclusions about familiar and unfamiliar scientific situations.
- You must be able to plan a scientific task, such as a practical investigation or experiment, to test an idea, answer a question or solve a problem.
- You must show that you understand how decisions are made about science and technology in different situations, including those which raise **ethical issues**
- You must be able to **evaluate** the impact of scientific developments or processes on individuals, communities or the environment.

Assessment Objective 3: Practical enquiry and data-handling skills

- You must be able to carry out practical tasks safely and skilfully.
- You must be able to **evaluate** your methods when collecting **first-hand** and **secondary data**.
- You must be able to **analyse** and **interpret** **qualitative** and **quantitative** data from different sources.

You must show that you have considered the **validity** and **reliability** of data in presenting and **justifying** conclusions.

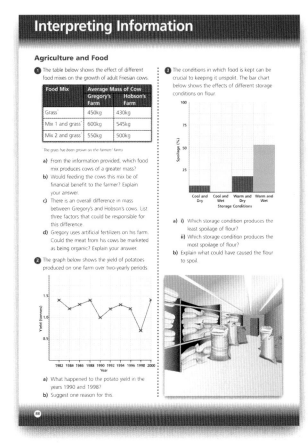

Practice applying your scientific knowledge

Check your answers

Interpreting Information

Agriculture and Food

1 The table below shows the effect of different food mixes on the growth of adult Friesian cows.

Food Mix	Average Mass of Cow	
	Gregory's Farm	Hobson's Farm
Grass*	450kg	430kg
Mix 1 and grass*	600kg	545kg
Mix 2 and grass*	550kg	500kg

*The grass has been grown on the farmers' farms

a) From the information provided, which food mix produces cows of a greater mass?

b) Would feeding the cows this mix be of financial benefit to the farmer? Explain your answer.

c) There is an overall difference in mass between Gregory's and Hobson's cows. List three factors that could be responsible for this difference.

d) Gregory uses artificial fertilizers on his farm. Could the meat from his cows be marketed as being organic? Explain your answer.

2 The graph below shows the yield of potatoes produced on one farm over two-yearly periods.

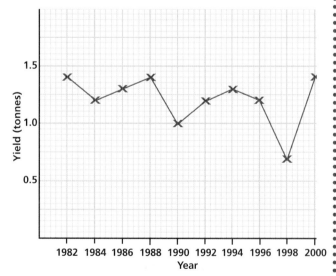

a) What happened to the potato yield in the years 1990 and 1998?

b) Suggest one reason for this.

3 The conditions in which food is kept can be crucial to keeping it unspoilt. The bar chart below shows the effects of different storage conditions on flour.

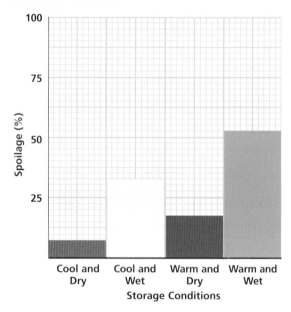

a) i) Which storage condition produces the least spoilage of flour?

 ii) Which storage condition produces the most spoilage of flour?

b) Explain what could have caused the flour to spoil.

Interpreting Information

Agriculture and Food (cont.)

4 A farmer currently grows intensively farmed arable crops and sells them at local food markets, and to a supplier who uses them for biofuel (a non-food use). The farmer has been informed that he will receive a subsidy if he grows organic crops.

a) Explain how the farmer will have to change his farming methods to switch from intensive to organic farming.

b) Would there be a financial benefit to the farmer in producing organic crops to sell at the market? Explain your answer.

c) Would there be a financial benefit to the farmer in producing organic crops to be used as a biofuel? Explain your answer.

5 The stages below show what happens in the production of sugar:

Stage 1: The sugar beet is dug out of the ground and washed.

Stage 2: The sugar beet is sliced into strips, and stewed in hot water. The sugar diffuses out of the strips into the water forming a 'sugar juice'.

Stage 3: The juice is cleaned and filtered to remove any other chemicals.

Stage 4: The juice is boiled. The water evaporates and a syrup remains.

Stage 5: The syrup is boiled to produce sugar crystals.

a) In Stage 2 the sugar beet is cut into strips. Why is it cut into strips rather than being left whole?

b) Why does sugar diffuse out of the strips?

6 The stages below show what happens in the production of cheese:

Stage 1: A milk mixture is created.

Stage 2: Rennet (containing the enzyme chymosin) and lactic-acid-producing bacteria are added to the mixture.

Stage 3: The lactic-acid-producing bacteria curdle the milk and convert the milk sugar into lactic acid. The chymosin causes the proteins in the milk to clump together.

Stage 4: The curd (solid) is separated from the whey (liquid).

Stage 5: The curd is transferred to moulds and the resulting cheese is pressed into its final shape.

a) Chymosin is an enzyme. What does an enzyme do?

b) How does the use of chymosin help to make the cheese production process more sustainable?

7 Biomass is the living mass of a biological material. In an experiment, two pots of yoghurt were left in different atmospheres for a week. Pot A was left in a hot, humid atmosphere and Pot B was left in a dark, cold atmosphere. At the end of the week, the biomass in each pot was tested. The results are shown below.

A 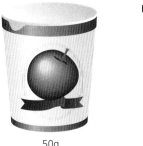 B

50g   27g

a) i) Which pot has a greater biomass?
   ii) Explain why this pot has a greater biomass.

b) Was this an accurate test? Explain your answer, giving at least two reasons.

Interpreting Information

Agriculture and Food (cont.)

8 The stages below show what happens in the processing of beef burgers:

> **Stage 1:** Cows reared and sent to market.

> **Stage 2:** Cows sent to slaughterhouse.

> **Stage 3:** Meat cut and minced. Made into quality beef burgers.

> **Stage 4:** Packaged and stored in freezer compartments in a warehouse.

> **Stage 5:** Delivered to supermarkets.

a) i) In this example, the meat from the cows is used to make beef burgers. Name one other product, apart from meat, that could be obtained from the slaughtered cow.

   ii) Is this an example of a gathered harvest, or a whole organism harvest?

b) There are many monetary costs involved in the production of meat products: rearing the animals, producing the product, etc. Are there any environmental costs? Explain your answer.

9 The following extract is from an article that describes an alternative fuel to petrol / diesel.

Lonsdale News   Tuesday, January 30

Cars powered by sugar!

Cars in the future could be powered by ethanol (better known as grain alcohol), a fuel that is easily distilled from sugar cane and is a cheap alternative to petrol and diesel.

Although alcohol releases less energy than petrol when it burns, scientists hope that the use of sugar cane will increase because it is cheaper to use than fossil fuels and produces less of the harmful gas, carbon dioxide, when it is burnt.

a) Petrol is produced from crude oil, and is a non-renewable energy source. Explain what a non-renewable energy source is.

b) If sugar can be used to produce fuel, what effect will this have on the price of sugar?

c) Why would using ethanol as a fuel be more sustainable than using petrol or diesel? Give two reasons.

HT **10** The graph alongside shows the effect of light intensity on the photosynthesis of a plant.

a) Explain what happens between points A and B on the graph.

b) i) What happens after point B? Explain why.

   ii) Name two other factors that could be affecting photosynthesis after point B.

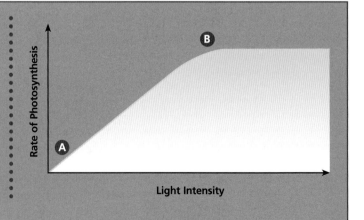

Scientific Detection

1 The pH scale below shows the acidity or alkalinity of different substances.

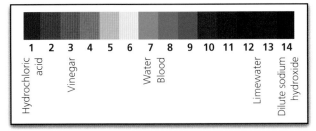

a) What is the pH of water?

b) What is the pH of limewater?

c) Which is the most acidic, hydrochloric acid or vinegar?

2 A patient tests the sugar levels in his urine by using a reagent strip. He then compares the colour on his strip against a standard chart.

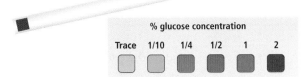

a) What does the colour of the reagent strip (shown above) indicate about the level of sugar in the patient's urine?

b) What condition might the patient have? Explain your answer.

3 A forensic scientist uses electrophoresis to analyse samples of DNA found at a crime scene against DNA samples taken from the victim and two suspects. The results are shown below.

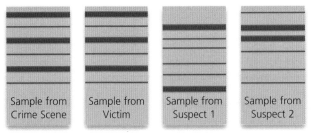

a) Could the blood sample from the crime scene be used as evidence that either of the suspects was present at the crime scene? Explain your answer.

b) Give one other use for electrophoresis.

4 The image below was taken with a light microscope. It shows a pollen cell.

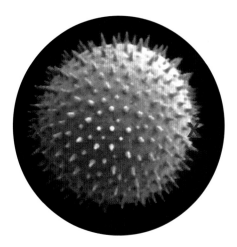

a) Suggest one feature that could be used to identify this type of pollen grain.

b) i) Measure the width of the pollen cell from the crosses marked.

ii) If the cell has been enlarged x40, calculate the actual size of the pollen cell.

5 The image below was taken with an electron microscope. It shows part of a strand of hair.

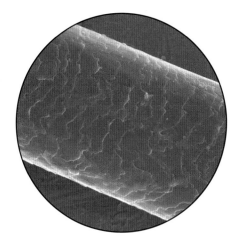

a) Suggest one feature that could be used to identify this hair strand.

b) The image has been magnified x600. If the width of the image of the hair is 1.08mm, what would be the actual width of the hair?

c) Give one advantage of using an electron microscope over a light microscope.

Interpreting Information

Harnessing Chemicals

1 Look at the pie chart below which shows production of chemicals in industry.

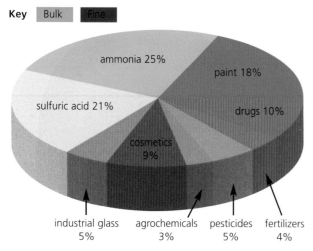

Key Bulk Fine

ammonia 25%
paint 18%
sulfuric acid 21%
drugs 10%
cosmetics 9%
industrial glass 5%
agrochemicals 3%
pesticides 5%
fertilizers 4%

a) From the information above, what percentage of chemicals produced by industry are fine chemicals?

b) Which chemical is produced in the largest quantity?

2 The graph below shows the results of the same chemical reaction under different conditions. The same amount and concentration of reactants is used in both reactions.

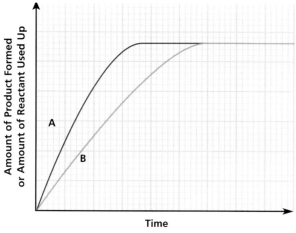

Amount of Product Formed or Amount of Reactant Used Up

A

B

Time

a) Both lines become horizontal at the top. What does this show?

b) Reaction A was faster than reaction B. Give three factors that could have affected the rate of reaction.

c) Which reaction, if any, formed more of the product? Explain your answer.

3 The information below gives details of a sustainable chemical process.

Ethanol is an important raw material found in fuels, paints, cosmetics and polymers. Ethanol can be produced by three different methods; the advantages and disadvantages are listed below:

Synthetic Method
- High energy usage.
- Toxic by-products produced.
- A purification stage is needed.
- Uses non-renewable raw materials.
- Ethene is converted to ethanol using steam and a catalyst.

Fermentation Method
- Uses renewable raw materials, e.g. sugar cane.
- Carbon-neutral process.
- Some household waste can be used to produce ethanol.
- Large areas of land are needed to grow specific crops as the raw materials.
- Only part of the plant material is used; the rest can be used to make animal feed stocks.
- Sugars are converted into ethanol and carbon dioxide.

Biotechnology Method
- Raw materials are waste biomass and not specifically grown for ethanol production.
- Genetically engineered *E.coli* bacteria are used to convert plant sugars into ethanol.
- Carbon-neutral process.

a) *The synthetic method is the least sustainable method of producing ethanol.* Give two examples from the text which support this statement.

b) Is fermentation or biotechnology the most sustainable method of producing ethanol? Explain your answer.

Harnessing Chemicals (cont.)

4 In an experiment 100cm³ hydrochloric acid is reacted with 10g calcium carbonate to make calcium chloride. The chemicals are sold to laboratories at the following prices:

hydrochloric acid
£8.40 per litre

calcium carbonate
£32.00 per kg

a) What is the cost of the hydrochloric acid that was used in the reaction above?

b) What is the cost of the calcium carbonate that was used in the reaction above?

5 Several types of sun cream with an advertised Sun Protection Factor of 16 were tested (see table below). To be approved for use they need to have the advertised amount of Sun Protection Factor (SPF) and cause no adverse effects.

a) Would Sun cream D be approved? Explain your answer.

b) Would Sun cream E be approved? Explain your answer.

c) What might happen if Sun cream C was approved and put on the market?

* Water resistance means the sun cream is still effective after a 20-minute swim.

HT **6** The table below shows the solubility of various chemicals. If solubility is below 1, the chemical is insoluble in water and can be made by precipitation. If the solubility is above 1, the chemical is soluble in water and cannot be made by precipitation.

Chemical	Formula	Solubility mol/dm³ 20°C
sodium carbonate	Na_2CO_3	0.66
calcium carbonate	$CaCO_3$	0.00013
zinc carbonate	$ZnCO_3$	0.00164
sodium sulfate	Na_2SO_4	0.303
zinc sulfate	$ZnSO_4$	3.56
sodium nitrate	$NaNO_3$	12.3
silver nitrate	$AgNO_3$	14.2
silver chloride	$AgCl$	0.0000153

a) Would silver chloride be made by the precipitation method?

b) Would sodium nitrate be made by the precipitation method?

Feature Being Tested	Sun Cream A	Sun Cream B	Sun Cream C	Sun Cream D	Sun Cream E
Flow	Hard to rub on (thin liquid)	Easy to rub on	Easy to rub on	Hard to rub on (thick liquid)	Easy to rub on
SPF	16	10	8	16	20
Reaction to Skin	No reaction	No reaction	No reaction	May irritate sensitive skin	No reaction
Resistance to Water*	Remains resistant for 5 minutes	Remains resistant for 40 minutes	Remains resistant for 40 minutes	Remains resistant for 60 minutes	Remains resistant for 35 minutes

Interpreting Information

Harnessing Chemicals (cont.)

7 The pie chart below shows the various industries in which inks and dyes are used:

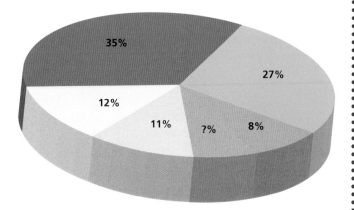

Key

- Commercial
- Printers
- Machinery
- Medicine
- Food Industry
- Textiles

a) What percentage of ink is used in medicine?

b) Which area of industry uses the second largest amount of ink?

8 A colour technologist is developing a range of different chemical dyes to use in a food product.

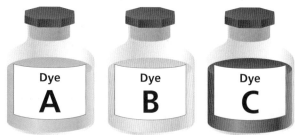

She carries out a range of different experiments to produce the dyes and then tests them. She finds the following results:

- Dye A contains an unknown substance.
- Dye B contains numerous known chemicals.
- Dye C is made from an organic substance.

a) Would Dye A be safe to use in a food product without further testing? Explain your answer.

b) Suggest two reasons why quality assurance tests need to be carried out.

9 The bar graph below shows the percentage of ingredients in four different toothpastes.

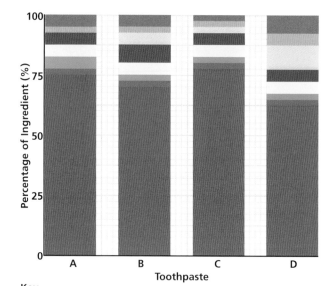

Key

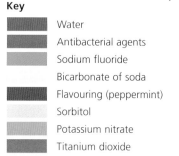

- Water
- Antibacterial agents
- Sodium fluoride
- Bicarbonate of soda
- Flavouring (peppermint)
- Sorbitol
- Potassium nitrate
- Titanium dioxide

Bicarbonate of soda and titanium dioxide are active ingredients which help to remove stains.

a) i) Which toothpaste would be the most effective at whitening teeth?

ii) Which toothpaste would be the least effective at whitening teeth?

b) Potassium nitrate is a sensitivity reducer. Which toothpaste would be the most effective at reducing sensitivity?

c) Sorbitol is a detergent added to make a toothpaste foam. Would there be a difference between the effectiveness of Toothpaste A and Toothpaste C at cleaning teeth?

d) A scientist recommends that children under 7 should not use a toothpaste which contains more than 7% sodium fluoride. Would the scientist recommend all the toothpastes in the chart to a child aged 6?

Interpreting Information

Materials and Performance

1 Pieces of wood can be joined together by different fastenings. Three different types of fastenings are detailed in Table 1 below.

a) Nick wants to make a cheap and practical bookcase to go in his bedroom. He is considering using rivets. Would they be suitable? Explain your answer.

b) Nick constructs a fence in his garden. Suggest a suitable type of fastening and explain the reason for your choice.

2 Table 2 details different materials that could be used for the base of a frying pan.

a) Would glass be a suitable material? Explain your answer.

b) Copper has two properties that would make it a suitable choice. What are they?

c) Give one disadvantage of choosing copper.

d) Give one advantage of choosing aluminium.

Communications

1 The flow chart below shows the process of data transmission for a digital radio.

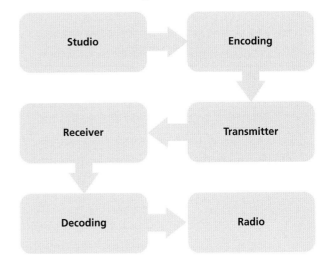

a) What is the output stage in the above flow chart?

b) Name two processor stages in the above flow chart.

Table 1

Fastening	Cost and Fitting	Effectiveness	Quality of Finish
Nuts and Bolts	Cheap parts, but holes need to be drilled to fit the fastenings	Secure fastening, but bolts are liable to snap under tension	High
Nails	Cheap parts and hammered into place	Quick and easy to fit, although it is the least secure method of fastening	Low (the nails are still visible)
Rivets	Expensive (requires drilling and welding to fit the fastening)	Very secure, lightweight and high strength	Very high

Table 2

Material	Thermal Conductivity (W/mk)	Melting Point (°C)	Stiffness (GPa)	Density (g/cm³)
Glass	1.5	1000	70	2.50
Copper	400.0	1085	130	8.95
Aluminium	237.0	660	70	2.70
Stainless steel	16.3	1400	200	7.90

Answers and Comments

Agriculture and Food

1 a) The combination of Mix 1 and grass.
This information can be deduced from the table.

b) Yes. A heavier (i.e. larger) cow would produce a greater yield of meat which would mean a greater profit for the farmer.
You need to understand the economic benefits of different yields of products.

c) Living conditions, e.g. temperature and shelter; having a clean supply of water; the quality of the grass.
You need to use and apply your knowledge of the factors that can affect the growth of animals. The question asks for three factors so make sure you give three in order to gain the maximum marks.

d) Gregory uses artificial fertilizers, which means that he does not farm organically. The cows would eat the grass he produces and, therefore, their meat could not be considered to be organic.
You need to understand the differences between organic and intensive farming methods, and apply this knowledge.

2 a) The yield dropped.
This information can be determined by looking at the graph.

b) Accept any suitable answer such as: drought or disease.
This question requires you to use your knowledge about the factors that affect the growth of plants.

3 a) i) Cool and dry.
ii) Warm and wet.
Both these questions can be answered by interpreting the information in the graph.

b) The growth of microorganisms.
You need to apply your knowledge of what causes food to go off.

4 a) He will have to stop using artificial pesticides and fertilizers.
You need to understand the differences between organic and intensive farming methods.

b) Yes. He would receive a subsidy.

c) No, the organic crops would cost him more to produce and the added quality factor would not make any difference to the selling price for a non-consumable crop.
You need to understand and apply your knowledge of the costs and benefits of organic farming.

5 a) The strips create a larger surface area for the sugar to diffuse out of.
This question is testing your background scientific knowledge.

b) The sugar particles move from a high concentration to a low concentration because of a difference in concentration.
You need to recall what diffusion is.

6 a) An enzyme speeds up the rate of a chemical reaction.

b) It increases the rate of reaction but is not used up itself. It can therefore be re-used.
You need to recall your knowledge of enzymes and how they work.

7 a) i) Pot A.
You need to compare the results given.

ii) Microorganisms grow more quickly in a hot, humid temperature.
You need to know the optimum conditions for microorganism growth.

b) No. There are many factors that you do not know, for example, whether the biomass in each pot was the same at the beginning of the experiment or whether each pot contained the same amount or type of yoghurt.
You need to apply your knowledge of experiments and what makes a fair test.

Answers and Comments

Agriculture and Food (cont.)

8 a) i) Accept either: leather OR bonemeal fertilizer.
You need to recall the other uses of organisms in whole organism harvests.

ii) This is an example of a whole organism harvest.
You need to use your knowledge of the different ways in which organisms are harvested to answer this question.

b) Yes. An environmental cost might be the pollutants caused at the processing and transportation stages.
You need to apply your knowledge of pollutants and the factors affecting the environment.

9 a) It is an energy source that cannot be replaced within a lifetime.
You need to recall your knowledge of what a non-renewable energy source is.

b) The price of sugar will go up.
You can answer this question by applying the information given in the article.

c) Accept any suitable answer such as: sugar is a renewable energy source and can, therefore, be replaced. It also has less of a negative environmental effect.
You need to apply your knowledge of what sustainable energy is.

10 a) The increase in light intensity is causing photosynthesis to increase at a steady rate.
This question is testing your interpretation of the graph.

b) i) The rate of photosynthesis remains constant. The increasing light intensity has no further effect on photosynthesis.
You need to make sure that you clearly explain what happens, and why.

ii) Accept any two from: temperature, carbon dioxide, nutrients from the growing medium.
You need to know the other factors that limit the rate of photosynthesis.

Scientific Detection

1 a) pH 7

b) pH 12.5

c) Hydrochloric acid is the most acidic.
These questions can all be answered by interpreting the information provided.

2 a) High sugar levels.
The information is given in the question.

b) Diabetes, because diabetics have to test their blood sugar levels.

3 a) No, it is the DNA from the victim that matches the sample.

b) Accept any suitable answer such as: paternity testing.
You need to recall the uses of electrophoresis.

4 a) Accept any suitable answer, such as shape.

b) i) 43mm

ii) 1.075mm

5 a) Accept any suitable answer such as: scales.

b) 0.0018mm

c) Accept any suitable answer such as: greater magnification

Harnessing Chemicals

1 a) 36%

b) Ammonia at 25%
These answers can all be determined by looking at the information supplied in the pie chart.

2 a) This shows that the reaction has stopped.
You need to understand and apply the information given.

b) A catalyst; higher temperature; smaller particles.
You need to apply your knowledge of the factors affecting reactions.

c) Neither, they both formed the same amount, as the graph shows the flat line at the same value.
To answer this question you need to apply your knowledge of what happens during a chemical reaction.

Answers and Comments

Harnessing Chemicals (cont.)

3 a) It uses non-renewable raw materials. The process requires a large amount of energy which may come from burning fossil fuels, which results in large amounts of CO_2 emissions. Valuable, non-renewable resources are being used up.
You need to understand what sustainability is, and use and interpret the information from the text.

b) Biotechnology is the most sustainable. It uses waste products as the raw materials, so no materials are produced in order to make the ethanol.
You need to understand and interpret the information given.

4 a) 84p
$100cm^3$ is $\frac{1}{10}$ litre
therefore $\frac{8.4}{10}$ = £0.84 = 84p.

b) 32p
£32.00 per 1000g = 3.2p per gram. We want 10g, therefore 3.2p / gram x 10 = 32p. You need to know how to work out the basic cost of chemicals.

5 a) No, it may irritate sensitive skin.
b) Yes, it has the correct sun protection factor and does not cause any skin reactions.
Questions a) and b) can be answered by interpreting the information given.

c) Sun cream C has an actual sun protection factor that is lower than advertised. If this was used there is the chance that people could get burnt by the Sun, increasing their risk of getting skin cancer.
You need to apply your knowledge of the dangers of UV light.

6 a) Yes
b) No
You need to interpret the information supplied.

7 a) 7%
b) Printers (27%)
These questions can both be answered by looking at the information provided.

8 a) No, because the effects of the dye might not be known.
You need to interpret the information given and apply your knowledge.

b) To protect consumers; to ensure conformity to national and international standards.
You need to apply your knowledge of the quality control tests on product formulations.

9 a) i) Toothpaste D
ii) Toothpaste C
b) Toothpaste D
c) Both toothpastes would be equally effective.
d) Yes, because no toothpaste contains more than 7% sodium fluoride.
These questions can be answered by interpreting the information given.

Materials and Performance

1 a) No, they would be too expensive for what he requires.
b) Nails, as they can easily be hammered into place, and it does not matter if they are visible.
These questions can both be answered by interpreting the information in the table.

2 a) No. Glass does not conduct heat well.
b) Copper is a good conductor of heat and it has a high melting point.
c) It is very dense so it would be heavy to use.
d) It has a low density.
These questions can all be answered by interpreting the information given in the table.

Communications

1 a) Radio
b) Accept any two of the following: encoding, transmitter, receiver, decoding.

Notes

Index

Index

Acknowledgements

Author Information

Dr Dorothy Warren, is a member of the Royal Society of Chemistry, a former science teacher, and a Secondary Science Consultant with the Quality & Improvement Service for North Yorkshire County Council. Having been involved in the pilot scheme for Twenty First Century Science, she has an excellent understanding of the new specifications, which she is helping to implement in local schools.

Dr Eliot Attridge is a full member of the Institute of Biology, a chartered biologist CBiol, and an experienced Head of Science. He works closely with the exam board as an Assistant Examiner for Twenty First Century Science and was involved in writing the scheme of work for the new GCSE. His school, having been involved in the pilot, is now implementing the new GCSE.

Nathan Goodman has an in-depth understanding of the new science specifications, thanks to his roles as Secondary Science Strategy Consultant for North East Lincolnshire LEA and Regional Coordinator at the Institute of Physics for the physics teacher network. As an Assistant Headteacher, Nathan is involved in improving the teaching and learning of science at his current school.

Every effort has been made to contact the holders of copyright material, but if any have been inadvertently overlooked, the publisher will be pleased to make the necessary arrangements at the first opportunity.

The authors and publisher would like to thank everyone who contributed images to this book:

IFC	©iStockphoto.com / Andrei Tchernov
p.10	©iStockphoto.com / Nicholas Belton
p.10	©2004 Drs. Gary Glover and Lara Foland, Stanford University, Function BIRN
p.17	©iStockphoto.com / Patrick Hermans
p.42	©iStockphoto.com / Peter Galbraith
p.52	©iStockphoto.com / Laura Neal
p.70	©iStockphoto.com / Dawn Hudson
p.83	©iStockphoto.com / Helle Bro Clemmensen
p.87	©iStockphoto.com / Justin Welzien
p.103	©iStockphoto.com / Dane Wirtzfeld

ISBN 978-1-905129-71-3

Published by Letts and Lonsdale.

Project Editor: Charlotte Christensen

Cover and concept design: Sarah Duxbury

Designer: Ian Wrigley

Artwork: HL Studios

Letts and Lonsdale make every effort to ensure that all paper used in our books is made from wood pulp obtained from well-managed forests.

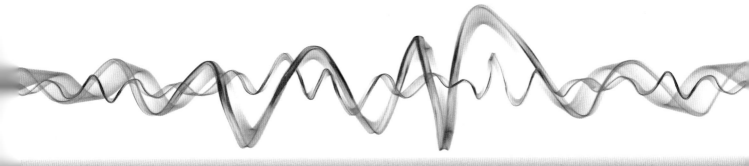

Periodic Table

Key

| relative atomic mass |
| **atomic symbol** |
| name |
| atomic (proton) number |

Example:
1
H
hydrogen
1

1	2												3	4	5	6	7	0
																		4 **He** helium 2
7 **Li** lithium 3	9 **Be** beryllium 4												11 **B** boron 5	12 **C** carbon 6	14 **N** nitrogen 7	16 **O** oxygen 8	19 **F** fluorine 9	20 **Ne** neon 10
23 **Na** sodium 11	24 **Mg** magnesium 12												27 **Al** aluminium 13	28 **Si** silicon 14	31 **P** phosphorus 15	32 **S** sulfur 16	35.5 **Cl** chlorine 17	40 **Ar** argon 18
39 **K** potassium 19	40 **Ca** calcium 20	45 **Sc** scandium 21	48 **Ti** titanium 22	51 **V** vanadium 23	52 **Cr** chromium 24	55 **Mn** manganese 25	56 **Fe** iron 26	59 **Co** cobalt 27	59 **Ni** nickel 28	63.5 **Cu** copper 29	65 **Zn** zinc 30		70 **Ga** gallium 31	73 **Ge** germanium 32	75 **As** arsenic 33	79 **Se** selenium 34	80 **Br** bromine 35	84 **Kr** krypton 36
85 **Rb** rubidium 37	88 **Sr** strontium 38	89 **Y** yttrium 39	91 **Zr** zirconium 40	93 **Nb** niobium 41	96 **Mo** molybdenum 42	[98] **Tc** technetium 43	101 **Ru** ruthenium 44	103 **Rh** rhodium 45	106 **Pd** palladium 46	108 **Ag** silver 47	112 **Cd** cadmium 48		115 **In** indium 49	119 **Sn** tin 50	122 **Sb** antimony 51	128 **Te** tellurium 52	127 **I** iodine 53	131 **Xe** xenon 54
133 **Cs** caesium 55	137 **Ba** barium 56	139 **La*** lanthanum 57	178 **Hf** hafnium 72	181 **Ta** tantalum 73	184 **W** tungsten 74	186 **Re** rhenium 75	190 **Os** osmium 76	192 **Ir** iridium 77	195 **Pt** platinum 78	197 **Au** gold 79	201 **Hg** mercury 80		204 **Tl** thallium 81	207 **Pb** lead 82	209 **Bi** bismuth 83	[209] **Po** polonium 84	[210] **At** astatine 85	[222] **Rn** radon 86
[223] **Fr** francium 87	[226] **Ra** radium 88	[227] **Ac*** actinium 89	[261] **Rf** rutherfordium 104	[262] **Db** dubnium 105	[266] **Sg** seaborgium 106	[264] **Bh** bohrium 107	[277] **Hs** hassium 108	[268] **Mt** meitnerium 109	[271] **Ds** darmstadtium 110	[272] **Rg** roentgenium 111								

Elements with atomic numbers 112–116 have been reported but not fully authenticated

*The Lanthanoids (atomic numbers 58–71) and the Actinoids (atomic numbers 90–103) have been omitted.

The relative atomic masses of copper and chlorine have not been rounded to the nearest whole number.